Bill Nighy

Bill Nighy

THE UNAUTHORISED BIOGRAPHY

SUE BLACKHALL

JB

JOHN BLAKE

Published by John Blake Publishing Ltd,
3 Bramber Court, 2 Bramber Road,
London W14 9PB, England

www.johnblakepublishing.co.uk

First published in hardback in 2010

ISBN: 978 1 84454 867 5

British Library Cataloguing-in-Publication Data:

A catalogue record for this book is available from the British Library.

Design by www.envydesign.co.uk

Printed in the UK by CPI William Clowes, Beccles, NR34 7TL

1 3 5 7 9 10 8 6 4 2

Contents

Introduction

A bit of a rough diamond in his early days, then there was the metamorphosis into a gem of a character actor. Now Bill Nighy is well and truly a national treasure. He is also somewhat eccentric and certainly enigmatic. Who would choose a career that puts you at the mercy of a critical public and sees you taking centre stage if you are a mass of anxieties, riddled with self-doubt, and hate being the focus of attention?

But Bill Nighy did just that, beating personal demons along the way to emerge as one of Britain's greatest acting stars and a multi-award winner. Of course, the film that finally made the world sit up and take notice was *Love Actually*, the biggest box-office hit of 2003. He was lauded for his performance as washed-up singer Billy Mack, scooping three awards. There were awards too for *I Capture the Castle* and the TV mini-series *State of Play* (also 2003), and for the 2005 TV film *Gideon's Daughter*, as well as thunderous applause for his 2006 Broadway appearance in *The Vertical Hour*.

His bemused frustration at the public's belief that until *Love Actually* he was not really doing much at all is understandable. In fact, Bill Nighy was quietly winning stage awards (an Olivier Award for Best Stage Actor for *Blue/Orange* in 2001 and the Barclays Theatre Award for best stage actor for *Skylight* way back in 1996). There were also awards for *Still Crazy* (1998), *The Lost Prince* and *The Young Visiters* (both 2003) and *Lawless Heart* (2001), plus numerous nominations. Long before audiences saw him as Billy Mack, he was a winner – he was just quietly biding his time and waiting for the right moment for recognition. Fame may have arrived late, but it came with a vengeance.

Self-effacing, funny and avoiding all the traditional techniques and clichés of his chosen career, Bill Nighy is anything but an actor's actor. He refuses to take his profession too seriously and has now conquered his fears well enough to find it all fun.

It was only while researching this book that I discovered just how much he is loved: he has been described as 'God' and the 'thinking woman's crumpet' (although he himself feels 'drinking woman's crumpet' is more apt!). Languid, lolloping, lanky and with limbs that appear to have a mind of their own, in front of the camera and away from it, he has endeared himself to us all. Then there is that trademark cut-glass voice that makes humorous lines even funnier, poignant words darker, and caustic comments turned in on himself memorable. And, as he celebrates his 60th year, perhaps he deserves one very special award – simply for being Bill Nighy.

Chapter One

Making an Entrance

The smells of childhood still bring back memories for Bill Nighy, but in his case it's not the salt of the sea, the scent of grass or indeed cooking aromas wafting from a kitchen. Instead, petrol is the most evocative smell. The start in life for one of Britain's best-loved and most revered stars was anything but auspicious. His family lived 'above the shop', in a flat that came with his father's job as garage manager. As he recalls, 'When you opened the door there were petrol pumps. The big smells of my childhood were Swarfega, oil and Marmite sandwiches.'

Back then, however, the only creative influence in his life was a resident inventor in a shed, who dedicated his life to dreaming up devices that would stop petrol being siphoned off. That was his childhood. But to be fair, the family did not balk when their somewhat wayward teenage son finally announced that he wanted to become an actor.

'My parents were a bit stunned but they were actually quite classy – they didn't panic,' he recalls.

He was born William Francis Nighy on 12 December 1949 in Caterham, Surrey. The surname has always caused him problems, with many insisting on pronouncing the 'y' when he himself would much prefer it be kept silent. The origins of 'Nighy' are a little hazy, although he once believed that it came from Hungary, appearing in the form of 'Nagy'. He shared his home and its less-than-aromatic scent with his father, Alfred Martin, who hailed from a Croydon family of chimney sweeps (later he left the business to become a garage owner), his Catholic Irish mother Catherine Josephine (a psychiatric nurse) and elder siblings, Martin and Anna. There were quite large age gaps between the three children, but Bill would later tell how his siblings looked out for him. He in turn became protective of both his brother and sister, refusing to talk about them when fame first struck, but he has revealed that he is delighted that they share his love of reading and the theatre.

Catherine and Alfred – 'two very decent people' – married in 1938. Bill loves to tell how his father, 'a quiet, elegant man, not famous for his dancing, still claimed my mother's heart above all others and she, by all accounts, could really move.' This was not an easy courtship, for the parish priest would shadow the pair to discourage their 'outside-the-faith' romance. However, 'It did not deter my father and they sought – and were given – a special dispensation from Rome, which was what was required then,' explains Bill.

He was an insecure child, a trait not helped by the inheritance, from his mother's side, of the condition Dupuytren's contracture (named after Baron Guillaume Dupuytren, the surgeon who developed an operation to correct the affliction), in which the ring finger and little finger of each hand bend inwards towards the palm. This condition can be treated with surgery, but sadly the results are not always satisfactory. It is a little strange, however, that Bill has not pursued some of the newer, alternative treatments – especially as the condition worsens with age.

One can only imagine Bill's childhood agony as he endured the taunts of 'Nerves' – short for 'nervous' because of his shyness and awkwardness – 'Being called "Nerve" sounds cool until you know what it is short for' – and 'Knucks', a reference to his misshapen knuckles. No wonder he has described himself as being shy in those days, preferring to spend time on his own. Today, however, he is happy to talk about his 'funny hands'.

They were to prove a handicap when he embarked on a brief flirtation with making music. 'I know some guitar players who have had the same condition and they find it deeply irritating,' he once said. 'There are two glamorous facts about it: it only affects people with Viking blood and Frank Sinatra had it in one hand.' He often jokes about his affliction, claiming some believe that he belongs to a 'secret lodge' when he shakes their hand and two of his fingers go into their palm: 'Women can think I'm making some sort of vulgar gesture so I try not to shake people's hand, or I explain that I suffer from this hand problem.' Small consolation perhaps, but fellow sufferers include Samuel Beckett, Ronald Reagan and Margaret Thatcher.

Being of part-Irish stock, he was raised as a Catholic and served as an altar boy. It was only natural that he should attend a Catholic school and aged five he entered the St Francis of Assisi Primary School in Caterham. As an older boy, Bill used to serve Mass at school twice a week. 'That meant you had to fast overnight, so that your body was available for the body of Christ. And after you'd served, you didn't have to work in your first lesson, and you could sit there, in class, in front of everyone else, having a cup of tea and a Marmite sandwich' (hence Marmite being one of Bill's ever-lasting childhood memories). Bill gave up being a practising Catholic at around the age of 15 when he started 'combing my hair and worrying about my trousers'. He would be the first to admit that although he was a bright little boy – as well as a 'minor nuisance', he was never going to achieve academic success. At the time, acting didn't enter his thoughts as something that he might one day prove to be successful at. As a child he only went to the theatre twice, one of those occasions being to see a Brian Rix farce on his father's works outing.

Having been marked as a 'borderline case' after taking his 11-plus, Bill was invited for a sort of entrance exam at the all-boys' grammar, John Fisher

School in Purley, to decide whether he was of a standard to attend grammar school. He was encouraged by the kindly head teacher to bring along any projects of which he was particularly proud. This could be anything, he was told – perhaps a painting or two he had done at home, maybe a poem or story. It should have prompted Bill, with his desire to please, to prove his worth. Instead, he chose to dream and worry, with his father ultimately forcing him to take along an almost complete colour-by-numbers book in a bid to demonstrate some creativity in his child.

'I knew nothing about anything but was too thick to realise it,' Bill later admitted. 'Looking back, I think such ignorance made me try.'

Somehow, he managed to make it into the John Fisher School, an institution with a strong Catholic ethos that was keen to promote Christian values and produce outstanding students. While not exactly shining, Bill did display some of the star qualities that would later win him huge acclaim in the acting world. He joined the school's theatre group and was, fortunately for him, too tall to be one of the boys chosen to play the female roles. Still, the idea of earning a living as an actor had not yet occurred to him – it didn't seem right for a gawky kid with so many neuroses. Years later he summed up his incredulity that anyone like him could ever perform in public: 'If you had to look at a gang of kids and decide which one was going to be an actor, you would look for the kid who was cowering in the corner, looking paranoid and self-conscious, and worrying about where to put his left hand. You'd think, "Yep, we'll have him, he'll do."'

Despite the confidence he must have needed to tread the boards on the school stage, Bill did not have a wonderfully happy time there. He wasn't top of the class academically, but he did make an attempt at sports, with running being one of his favourites, although perhaps not for the right reasons.

'I was quite fast and used to do a bit of cross-country at school,' he recalls. 'I also used to run very fast at rugby because I was so allergic to the idea of physical contact with another boy. They would put me on the wing, so I used to run like blue murder just to keep out of trouble.' Most of the time, though, he suffered a loneliness and frustration that came out in one of his earliest writings. In true morose schoolboy style, Bill once penned a piece for the school magazine. Just 'boy stuff', as he once described it, but it revealed his feelings of alienation in a Catholic atmosphere that he found stifling. Some memories still haunt him: for example, there was the time when he was hauled to the front of the class because of the 'gunk' he had used to tame his wild teenage hair: 'The teacher pulled me by my hair saying, "Nighy, what horrible hair!" The whole class thought it was Christmas. I was called "Horrible Hair" after that.'

His hair was to make him 'look like Art Garfunkel' until he was in his twenties and it suddenly straightened. 'It's funny, I can't remember when it went back, yet it must have been one of the best days of my life,' he recalls. 'Even if it had been straight then, I would still have been disabled with self-consciousness.'

Grammar school was probably not the best environment for someone so lacking in confidence and without any real academic leanings. In fact, how he ever got a place at all is still a wonder to him: 'My friends all got a different bus in the opposite direction and you had to wear a hat, a blue cap. My dad didn't want me to go – he felt I'd be uncomfortable and he wasn't wrong...' One of his school reports summed him up as 'a dreamy boy, full of nonsense.' They were probably right. When he was 14, Bill took up his father's offer to paint his bedroom any colour he wanted. Bill chose red on one wall, purple on another and a lime green on a third – 'a disastrous first design decision'. True schoolboy dreams came by way of a poster of a famous model of the time, Celia Hammond, on the inside of his wardrobe.

It was enough to make him want to run away – and he did just that when he was 15. Bill and a school friend had the big idea of making it to the Persian Gulf, just because it sounded exotic. It was one of those crazy youthful impulses, with Bill later confessing: 'I hadn't a thought in my head... I just threw a suitcase out of the window. I could have used the front door, but I didn't want to run it past my dad. Bob [Dylan] calls it that highway sound. I was young, I just wanted to run – it's natural.'

They made it to France but running away took confidence, something shy Bill did not then have. The lads were 'hungry and skint' and Bill was eventually forced to call on the British Consulate in France for help. They in turn contacted his less-than-happy father, who sent him money to get home – with the insistence that no matter how long it took him, his son would have to repay the debt: 'The British consul shipped me home for 25 quid and I had to pay my father back. He was a wee bit cross. It was a great scandal in our family, obviously and it took me about three years to pay it off.'

Eventually he left school at 16 with no qualifications – 'I was in serious trouble. I went back home, went to school over the summer, flunked and didn't make it through the exams, which was unfortunate because as a result I didn't get what they call in England a 'further education'. Nothing would have given me more pleasure than to be given licence to read to some purpose.'

He did, however, have dreams of becoming a great writer. Just how he would make this happen, he wasn't sure. His father might have been happy, had Bill followed him into the car business – he was also a driving instructor, who once went round Brands Hatch in a supercharged Bentley.

Bill started his working life on the *Croydon Advertiser*, where he soon realised that he needed more than dreams to fulfil his ambition – at least five O-levels for a start – before he could begin his journalistic training. 'I wanted to be a journalist,' he was later to muse, 'Principally because Ernest Hemmingway had been a journalist and he was my hero. He had worked on the *Toronto Star* when he was 17 as a cub reporter, so I figured I would be like Ernest. I was very keen and really saw myself in a good hat and decent trench coat. I had the completely romantic vision of what a journalist was like.'

But with only a tea-making future to look forward to, he quit, his ambition to be a budding journalist – 'because I thought it was glamorous and that I'd meet beautiful women in the rain' – thwarted. Mrs Nighy, obviously a far more practical soul than her son, escorted him to the Employment Exchange. Undoubtedly there was much shaking of heads when the youngster was asked what he wanted to be and he replied, 'An author'. The member of staff who had the misfortune to have Bill sitting before him flicked through the sheaf of job vacancies on his desk before announcing that they didn't, at present, have any vacancies for authors.

'The bloke didn't panic – he just got a book and said, "No, I don't think we have any jobs for authors" and I said, "No, I didn't think you would,"' he recalls. He insists he wasn't trying to be funny with his answer but only admitted it to alert the job finder to his goal: 'I didn't expect him to get me a job authoring anywhere but when I said what I wanted to do, my mother pressed her foot on mine under the table as if to say, "You stupid sod". Bless her!'

His wish was only somewhat accommodated when he was granted a job as messenger boy at *The Field* magazine in Mayfair. It wasn't writing, but it was a living. He rode the streets of London in black cabs and got free tea and cheese rolls at the Dorchester Hotel during edition changes – plus money in his pocket, enabling young Bill to shape himself into a mod: 'I always liked suits. I was a mod, or at least I aspired to being a mod. There was a strain of mod-dom that was very classic, very witty, and very kind of faux conservative. The girls used to wear twinsets and pearls, and would have short bobs and no makeup – I used to think it was so sexy.' His first pay packet was spent on mohair sweaters and later ones on snappy suits, loafers and the Fred Perry shirts that completed his new image. 'Loud' just wasn't in his sartorial vocabulary – 'I tried to steer clear of paisley, frankly, or anything too floral. I was more like what they later called a Suedehead. It was basically Ben Sherman, John Smedley, mohair trousers and Madras jackets. I aspired to what they call "top mod-ness". There was a period of my life where I couldn't leave the house because I didn't have the right jeans. It was a quest and I was devout.'

He still purchases one of those early fashion passions, a John Smedley sweater, every year.

Bill might not have been writing, but he was certainly an avid reader even though there were few books at home – the collected works of Dickens that his dad had won in a competition in the *Daily Express*, and a world atlas amongst them – and Bill discovered the delights of second-hand book shops. Ernest

Hemingway, Henry Miller, Ford Maddox Ford and F. Scott Fitzgerald were among his literary heroes: 'The only big enthusiasm I had when I was young was books and reading. Many of these heroes had been in Paris in the twenties.' It was not long before he was keen to follow in their footsteps, and despite being offered the chance to train as a sub-editor on *The Field*, Bill chose to head for Paris with its promise of a Bohemian lifestyle so befitting that of a budding writing genius – 'I always had this dream that there would be this girl there too.'

Ultimately, there was to be little writing: 'I ended up begging on the streets and did not write a word.' He got so far as writing the title – *The Golden Calf* – and then drew a margin (for the teacher's comments): 'That was the saddest thing: it was either rather moving or pathetic. I drew the margin and then I sat there for a while and then I think the phone rang, and that was the end of my writing career. But what could I do? The phone rang and somebody called. I had to take the call...'

His escape to Paris wasn't the adventure he had anticipated. The first night he and his friends, brothers Brandon and Jamie Jenning, slept under the Arc de Triomphe, while Bill dreamt of being the next Hemingway, prepared to suffer for his art. (He was rudely awoken by traffic circulating around him). He even tried to follow in his hero's footsteps and go to war: 'I actually went to the Israeli embassy and tried to volunteer for the six-day war to try and be like Ernest, but they said you have to go for six months and I thought, hang on, I don't want to be *that* much like Ernest!' Even before he set foot on French soil, he was getting into character: 'I even rather grandly dropped my trousers on the beach at Folkestone, took off my underwear and threw it into the sea because I had read that my great literary hero, Ernest Hemingway, always went commando.'

It was also on the beach at Folkestone, Kent, that Bill smoked his first marijuana joint. 'It was with a bloke I had never seen before and I have never seen since. It was a big mistake and it made me feel sick, and if I'd had any sense I would have left it there. I didn't, but I don't do it anymore,' he would later recall. Dreaming about being a famous author didn't earn him money, though. Instead, he mixed with some of the more dubious characters of Paris, while no doubt wondering what life was all about, in between begging on the Trocadero – '*Avez-vous un franc pour moi?*' being the only phrase he knew – and weighing up his conscience about being a schoolboy 'gigolo'.

The owner of a brothel called Madame Cuckoo's told him that he could earn 200 francs if he slept with much older women. Bill confesses that he took time to work out just how many couplings he would have to undertake to earn enough for a Harley Davidson to hurtle through the streets before declining. He still ponders the offer to this very day: 'I used to count how many women I would have to sleep with to be able to afford a Harley Davidson because Paris was full of all these cool guys on Harleys, with their suits and shades. But I never did it. In my case, I had never done it – I did not know how to do it.'

Then still a virgin, the idea of sleeping with anyone at all, let alone for money, secretly terrified him. Even the liberating era of the so-called Swinging Sixties eluded him: 'I never had any sex in the sixties. I was always too shy and didn't want to take my top off. I have a difficult body – you don't want to see me with nothing on.' So unconfident was he in those early days that the thought of asking a girl to dance and being snubbed was enough to shake his already fragile self-esteem. 'It's awful being turned down for a dance when you are a young man. Then what are you going to do? Kill yourself!' he remarked, with his usual self-effacement.

In Paris, aged just 17, he was oblivious to the hurt and concern that he was causing his family back home. At one point he wrote to his father expressing a wish to be left to his own devices. It was only much later that he realised the pain his troubled schoolboy days caused those he left behind. He recalls: 'When I ran away, I wrote a letter to my father instructing him not to find me. After he died, I found it in his papers and it was arguably the most pompous and stupid thing I have ever read. It was a great regret to me by then – my father was a decent man.'

No book was to emerge from his self-inflicted time in the garrets of Paris, even though he could not have wished for a more conducive atmosphere in which to pursue his art. 'I did aspire to a Bohemian life – I wanted to live like a writer,' he reflected. 'I knew that was what I wanted from an early age, my mid-teens, probably. But

I didn't feel sure enough about myself to know what I was looking for. What could you call it, self-expression? I thought that sounded too posh. In other words, I was going to write beautiful, thrilling sentences that would break hearts and hopefully get me a girlfriend... I only got into acting because it was a similar lifestyle to writing, except you don't have to write. Someone else does that and you just have to fanny about. It sounded like you don't have to get up in the morning – which is a laugh, because if anyone has to get up in the morning, it's actors on film sets!' After three months, he returned home: 'I was an average mess.'

Writing, for the time being at least, was put on hold. He would later admit: 'I am a world-class procrastinator. I'm only an actor because I've been putting off being a writer for 35 years.' With the unsuccessful Parisian sojourn behind him, he returned to the far less glamorous environs of Croydon, where he took a number of jobs, including being a petrol pump attendant and cleaning at the hospital where his mother worked. It was the sixties, a time that might have been created just for him, apart from the almost obligatory message to 'get it on' with everybody. Somewhere out there was the something he wanted – he simply didn't know what it was. Then there was the virtually mandatory crack at being in a band, though they never made it beyond rehearsals.

Just as in all other areas of his life, he preferred escapism to the duller practicalities of being proactive. He felt his wild hair was a good attribute for any guitarist and he practised in front of the wardrobe mirror with a tennis racquet 'trying to throw a few moves that might suggest I could be good in bed – I saw that as my responsibility to the band. But I wasn't particularly good in bed and I didn't know what shapes to throw to show you were good in bed.'

He hoped he might get selected, but a rock'n'roll life was not to be. There were six in the band and they rehearsed in a garage: 'but we were all so self-conscious and damaged by it all that we never really saw the light of day. I found it all tremendously exposing, standing in front of a band and singing in a way that I never have done with acting. We never got out of the garage. I was also a keen air guitar player and was hoping that at some point I'd visit Finland, where the world championships are found each year. I thought I'd be the first air guitar player that actually takes time to tune the air guitar! They never tune it right...'

Being caught out playing air guitar, however, is not just a distant memory that makes him squirm today. He still does it... and is still caught out.

On one occasion, he was subjected to a rather intrusive search by a rubber-gloved police officer, but he blames himself: 'I was in Cornwall and a detective was crawling over my half of the tent, looking for drugs, and I was protesting that he was wasting his time...' He considered attention from the police to be an occupational hazard: 'There was nothing remarkable about it – you'd expect trouble.' Especially, he recalled, if you wore an Afghan coat: 'I never actually wore one, but I did know a man who did and that would get you nicked. Several of my friends were arrested for looking funny. And then it turned ugly – I got in the right car. If I'd got in the wrong car that could have been me and I could have served nine months in Brixton jail.'

Much the loner and prone to manic behaviour, Bill had a somewhat reclusive youth. Sometimes, there on his own, he would let rip, 'When I was young, the weather used to drive me mental. I used to have to contain myself in a better-than-any-drug-you-ever-took way. I used to scream and leap if the winds got high – and if there was rain attached to it, I'd become deranged. I used to run and jump in it, open my mouth, open my eyes, open my face to it... I dig it!'

During his most formative years, he sought solace in music. The Rolling Stones and Bob Dylan – especially Dylan, whose music he still loves today – were the artists who made him feel life had a reason. He didn't quite know what this might be, but so long as it was against the establishment and allowed him to live his life his way it was alright by him: 'I remember sitting in front of *Top of the Pops* and "Like a Rolling Stone" [one of Dylan's earliest songs] came on. I found it breathtaking. My dad just shook his head, it was beyond his comprehension.'

But Dylan, he says, changed his life: 'I left home on the strength of Dylan. His music was the trigger – it was something about the harmonica, that "mercury" sound, he called it. I used to hitchhike everywhere. I like being in between places.'

That almost unnerving empathy remains and not a single day goes by without him listening to the singer he idolises almost to obsession. 'If I'm in trouble, I go to Bob Dylan. And if I'm feeling really good, I go to Bob Dylan,' he once revealed. 'I don't know where I'd be without him, really. I'm never tired of listening to any of it.' For a while, music would be his reason for living in an otherwise uncertain existence. However, this passion was not something his father understood: 'I wanted him to understand because he was a good man and we would talk about music. We often had the Bing [Crosby] versus Frank [Sinatra] debate. He had two long-playing records, one of which was "White Christmas" by Bing, naturally. The other was the start of the Le Mans, which he would play me, counting through the sound of the gears. Not my mother's favourite record, she couldn't dance to that. But what I was into was too far, he couldn't get it. Now I am older, I can see why he didn't get it,' he was to admit, some forty years later, adding, 'it's funny, but at the time – 1966 – I just accepted that there was all this good music around. I thought that was the norm, but in retrospect I realise that it was an extraordinary time for music, extraordinary.'

His father, meanwhile, was happy enough with Bing – both his music and his casual style: 'My father had a style based on Bing Crosby. He liked the sports jackets and trousers, and that thing with the one hand in the trouser pocket. He used to smoke, so the other hand was busy.'

It's hard to emphasise just how important music was to Bill – and indeed still is today. When he was younger, it was the one thing that propelled him and gave his life meaning. It set a horizon which, however far away, he was determined to reach.

'Music presented a world of colour away from a grey world and I wanted to be in it. I wasn't very good at knowing what I wanted to do, but I was extremely good at knowing what I didn't want to do, and that was live in a world where you knew where everything was going to be in twenty-five years, where you knew how much you would be making and then you had to go to the same place every day.

'It's like being a gambler and when I was 18 that was music – I had a kind of ludicrous faith in the music between the guitar and harmonica of Dylan and it drove me nuts. I went all over Europe looking for something; the music was inspirational, records were exotic things. I had copies of soul imports from America, including one called "Um, Um, Um, Um, Um, Um" by Major Lance, which made me feel really good about myself. It's like that famous story of Keith Richards seeing Mick Jagger on Dartford railway station in Kent when they were both 17 and hardly knew each other, and Richards was drawn to Mick Jagger and had to go over to him because he was carrying a Chuck Berry album. Now a Chuck Berry album in Kent was unheard of, no one had the record. Now, of course, you can download anything, anywhere. In those days, it was a struggle.'

He would later go on to tell how it was believed that he and Keith Richards were good friends as Richards had enjoyed a cameo part in *Pirates of the Caribbean*: 'I had to say, "No, I just look like I'm a good friend of his..."'

He still suffered a chronic lack of self-confidence – even at 18 he preferred just walking on his own: 'I used to walk the dog a lot – that was how I tackled my self-consciousness. He was called Riff. It legitimised my late-night walks; I found it easier to be on my own.' It's hard to equate such introversion with a desire to bare one's soul in front of an audience, but a female friend studying to be a drama teacher tentatively suggested to Bill that he might like to try his hand at acting. He had also fallen for her and so naturally, he would have done anything she suggested: 'She could have said astronaut and I would've given it a stab, this is how deeply pathetic I was. I didn't know what audition meant – I thought it was a grant or something. I walked up the hill to this girl's house and said, "Look, I've got in." And she said, "No, it means you have to go down there and do an audition."'

It was his small success at the school drama club that encouraged him. He applied to the Guildford School of Drama and Dance (actually, he got his girlfriend to do this for him). His audition asked for one modern piece and a speech from Shakespeare. Accompanied by his friend Gavin, Bill went to a local library and stole the complete works of Shakespeare, carting it away in a carrier bag. He chose his two requisite three-minute audition pieces: a speech by Eliza Doolittle from Shaw's *Pygmalion* because he wanted to use his cockney accent and another by Cesario from *Twelfth Night* – not realising that Cesario is, in fact, the character Viola dressed as a man.

Despite the unwitting choice of two female readings (and only a thinly disguised ignorance of the fact), he was accepted 'by some miracle' into the school – known locally as the School of Murmur and Prance – and stayed there for two years. Not only was he surprised at being accepted, but also at being allowed to stay. He always felt they would find him out, later admitting: 'I never thought I would be an actor for very long, if at all – I was a bit of a dreamer. I just thought I would do acting for a while and see what happened until I thought of something else or actually faced the music and sat down and tried to write something. For quite a long time, I allowed the fantasy of writing to sustain me. It was always scheduled for some time other than now... But then jobs just got more interesting.'

Chapter Two

Acting the Part

Even the free-spirited world inhabited by drama students was unable to liberate the sexually repressed Bill Nighy. He admits that he was probably the only drama student who 'never got involved in any variation of sexual games. The younger generation thinks that everyone growing up in the 1960s must have had a hell of a time, but I didn't.'

He might not have got much action but he did manage to secure the lead in John Osborne's *Epitaph for George Dillon.* One of Osborne's earlier works, this encompasses some of his favourite themes, including vegetarianism and a hatred of religion. The play tells the story of Kate Elliott's unhappy suburban south London family and the domestic tangles when she decides to adopt George Dillon as a surrogate son. Dillon is an intelligent man unable to find his place in the world. The part, it seems, was tailor-made for Bill Nighy, but he was mortified when some of his old school friends turned up to watch. Not only did they arrive late but they were also enjoying the effects of 'chemically induced improvements' and made nuisances of themselves in the back row. At one point, the girl takes Dillon's hand and remarks how beautiful it is, like marble: 'The entire back row erupted. "Good ole Knucks!" Bastards.'

But Bill proved that uncertainty about oneself probably makes for a better actor: 'I'm not an introvert, not exactly. And shy doesn't quite cover it because that suggests a degree of arrogance, a mixture of extreme vanity and self-disgust. No, acting for me wasn't so much a matter of knowing what I wanted to do: it was more about knowing what I didn't want to do – and that was to work hard in a nine-to-five job. Now I come to think of it, when people warned me that there would be long periods out of work if I became an actor, I couldn't keep a straight face because that was exactly what I had in mind. Yeah, baby! That sounded like a result. And you could go around, saying: "I am an actor, but I'm not currently working." Result again!'

Bill is probably doing himself a great injustice here, yet he looks back on those drama school days as a time when nothing was certain in his professional future. Despite his rather flippant approach to his talents, he did know what he wanted: 'I never imagined the things happening to me that have happened to me. Your immediate ambition each time is to make the next step forward. When I was at drama school, my ambition was just to be considered an actor; I wanted it to be possible for someone to construct a sentence with my name and the word actor in it, quite casually. I just wanted to be accepted in a kind of community of actors without fuss. I didn't feel like an actor and I wasn't convinced that I could become one, just to be involved with good writers and not to be a nuisance on stage. I didn't want to be involved in things that were craven – in other words, bad writing; in other words, things that diminish our experience rather than enrich them. I didn't want to be involved in things that were tedious or embarrassing, or cynical or drab. I've been lucky, you know. I've been extremely lucky that I've been able to appear in things that were pretty good. I've done my share of the other kind.'

In 1968 Flower Power and the idea of sharing everything from baths to beds to bodies was at its height. Again, Bill admits to missing out at the very time when he could have enjoyed all the sexual freedom he wanted. He sniffs at the label 'Summer of Love': 'That is apparently what it was called. It won't have been a freak who came up with that description, it must have been a newspaper editor. I wish someone had told me it was the Summer of Love at the time because I don't think I was particularly promiscuous. I certainly thought everyone else was at it, though. It was another example of men getting away with it, as Martin Amis would say. We would always turn to our girlfriends, or the girls we wanted to sleep with and say, "Baby, be cool!" It was a scoundrel's remark, like, "Don't be paranoid."

He doesn't even feel comfortable wearing shorts. 'It was a tough time to be young, having to take your clothes off and be cool about it,' he recalls. 'I didn't have the shape, so nothing would have persuaded me to do it.'

In fact, he was pretty much a non-starter at this time as far as women were concerned. Many years later, he gave a revealing insight into his crippling lack of confidence to Aidan Smith on the *Scotsman*: 'Every young man finds the effort of moving his eyes from the carpet into those of another person pretty difficult between the ages of 15 and 23. If they happened to be the eyes of a woman, I was disabled. I used to shave on tiptoe in order not to have to look in the bathroom mirror; I was allergic to the sight of myself.' Bill said he got good at not only reading people's minds but writing them too, as he mentally assessed what they were thinking about him. 'I assumed people took one look at me and went, "Oh, my God!" I reckoned that the bloke standing next to me was almost certainly in better shape than I was. Women, I decided, found me forgettable. And it wasn't just about looks. If they knew what I was really like, I'd say to myself, how lame and stupid I really was. That was a bad habit I got into – it was a fearful thing, I was pre-empting their disdain. Lately, I haven't had to worry too much, thank God. I look in the mirror now and go, "You silly old tosser!"'

The opposite sex was both a mystery and a threat to the young Bill. He just knew that somewhere along the line his mind turned to women. But he was so self-conscious that often he couldn't get up and walk across a room to go to the toilet because he couldn't think of 'anything cool to say on the way...'

After leaving Guildford in 1969 he took the traditional would-be actor's route into 'rep'. His first appearance, just six lines, was in Tennessee Williams' *The Milk Train Doesn't Stop Here Anymore* at the Watermill Theatre on the banks of the River Lambourn in Newbury. Early theatre credits simply list him as a 'performer'. In fact, he was multi-functional: putting up the set, doing the donkey work *and* acting. American actress Marcella Markham – then in her forties and no doubt a picture of intimidating glamour in high heels, sunglasses and fur coat – took a shine to the young Bill. And he was frightened. 'She also had that look, as if she wasn't wearing anything under the coat. I was terrified.'

But Markham took the stage with Bill and gave him a much-needed confidence boost. 'We were supposed to rehearse together. I was so intensely self-conscious that I could hardly get the words out and I wondered if I should be doing this at all. I did my lines and she did not respond. The silence went on for so long that I had invented a parallel universe to hide in. She looked at me for a long time and I expected her to say, "Bring me a real actor." Instead, in an act of tremendous kindness which I have never forgotten, she said to the director, "Where did you find him? The kid's fantastic!"

'Well, the kid was far from fantastic. She saw a lanky boy, frightened out of his wits, but this was one of the kindest things that anyone has ever done for me. She could have seen me off and probably ended my career in one remark, yet this was probably one of my biggest breaks. The message is: don't readily put young people down – give them a chance.'

Some time later, he went on to explain his defence mechanism – his self-created 'hostile universe'. It is his way of countering the actor's development of a 'process' (to which a bemused Bill often refers) and is his 'bubble' in which he exists while performing: 'It's a sort of joke that I have used, but it's also true. I think it's not a very good joke, but it's funny because it's true. The expression I've used is that I, instead of having a process, what I, in fact, do is I invent a hostile parallel universe and I live in it for a while. And in the hostile parallel universe, I'm usually about to get fired.

'It's not uncommon – you'd be surprised. Actors for the most part have exactly the same reaction to the prospect of appearing in public and being the only ones to speak, as does anyone else, which is pretty much, "Can I go home now? Could you call me a cab?" or words to that effect, you know? So, it's not just me. A lot of people do have similar experiences. Acting is what you do after you get the wind up. You know, in my universe there are a lot of people that are probably more justified or just in better shape.'

He had to lose his hippy look for his part in the Williams play, which could not have come at a worst time as he headed for the 1970 Isle of Wight Festival (headlined by Jimi Hendrix in his last live performance before his death that same year) with a very smart short-back-and-sides, which made him stand out from the rest of the long-haired revellers: 'It was like social death. The crowd would part, literally, as you walked along, because they assumed you were a policeman or in the armed forces, neither of which was going to get you laid in those days.'

That same year he had a small role as a character called William in the BBC's *Play for Today* series. He was in excellent company with the likes of David Threlfall, Miriam Margoyles, Mel Smith, John Gielgud, Jim Broadbent, Ian Holm, Bob Hoskins, Edward Woodward, Rupert Everett, David Suchet, Kenneth Branagh, Pete Postlethwaite, Anthony Hopkins, Pierce Brosnan, John Hurt, Michael Gambon and Ray Winstone all appearing in the dramas.

In 1971, Bill appeared at Edinburgh's Traverse Theatre in Olwen Wymark's *Speak Now*, which he later described as his first full acting job where he didn't have to drive the van (a reference to his travelling theatre days). Then followed a spell at the Cambridge Arts Theatre, including a run of Joe Orton's *Entertaining Mr Sloane* (in which he played Sloane) and appearances at Chester's Gateway Theatre in *Landscape and Silence*, two one-act plays by Harold Pinter. These were lowly, though happy, days for him, simply because he was doing something he felt he was halfway good at, though he still lacked the confidence of his contemporaries.

In the early seventies, he worked for the Everyman Theatre Company in Liverpool. 'Worked' is the word to use here, as Bill did not enjoy the luxury of being a full-time actor. He did all the odd jobs too, including serving behind the theatre bar, costume design and even a stint mending broken theatre seats, but he has fond memories of his three years with the theatre. Not only was he working alongside those who, like him, would become household names on screen, such as Pete Postlethwaite, Alison Steadman, Bernard Hill, Julie Walters, Trevor Eve and Jonathan Pryce, but he got to know the acclaimed Liverpudlian writers Willy Russell and Alan Bleasdale too.

'That's when I suppose I began to take it seriously,' he recalls. 'There was this very distinguished group of actors and eminent writers and they were all so committed to the community around; they were all so politically aware and funny and I started to get interested. Because I was in that kind of company I had to raise my game – I couldn't fake it quite the way I had been. I couldn't stand very still and do nothing and hope it was mistaken for having an internal life, or look moody and hope they would think it was something else.'

The Everyman was a converted chapel on Hope Street, a venue that had seen better days, and which still had gas lighting in the corridors and toilets. The walls were covered in the graffiti of well-known Liverpool poets. Downstairs, the bar menu boasted such exotic treats as chilli con carne and Bertorelli's ice cream, washed down with Newcastle Brown Ale.

As well as working alongside Jonathan Pryce, Bill worked under his direction too. He appeared as Skinnwe in Brian Friel's *Freedom of the City*, inspired by the Bloody Sunday incident of 1972, in which three people are thrown together by the tragic events of the day: a mother with 11 children, an idealistic student and Bill's somewhat typecast, cynical drifter, Skinnwe. In a controversial ending, all three are shot by the armed forces. At one performance, a bomb threat meant actor Kevin Lloyd had to ask the audience to leave the hall. They thought this was part of the show and laughed.

Another strong production was Chris Bond's *Under New Management*, in which Bill played a character called Harold. It was set around the closure of the Fisher-Bendix plant in Kirby, near Liverpool, in 1971, with 600 job losses.

Bill's time with the Everyman also presented the opportunity to be part of a travelling drama group called 'Van Load' with playwright David Hare. Theirs was a personal and professional relationship that would endure. Bill describes Hare as perhaps the most influential guide in his acting life: 'Working with David Hare has been as important as anything else. Working with him as a writer, but also working with him as a director, because he directed me on four occasions, during a very particular time in my life. In terms of loyalty, encouraging me and helping me to act, practically speaking, he is the most important person because he gave me leading roles for the first time.

He gave me leading roles on television and he gave me a leading role in the theatre, so that was the first big shift.

'When I first met David, it was the first time I had ever actually been asked to deliver lines. I recognised it as something that was beautiful and close to my heart. He expressed the world in a way I was very, very grateful for. And that was perhaps when I really, really began to take it seriously. I loved to have David direct me and some of my fondest memories are being in the rehearsal room with him and just laughing with David because he is a very funny guy. But because the plays were so fabulous and everything was so wittily and so elegantly put, I got the chance to say stuff that I truly believed in out loud in front of a thousand people every night. It was a new experience for me and it was a big part of me. It got my attention and made me think perhaps this is something I can do.'

Van Load managed to squeeze in up to 10 productions a year, playing at a variety of venues, like supermarkets, jails, schools, army camps and church halls. One such production was Willy Russell's *Sam O'Shanker*, a Robert Burns tale reset in present-day Liverpool, with the hero's horse replaced by a battered Ford Escort van. The somewhat edgy and experimental drama suited Bill. It also gave him licence to shock without feeling bad about it. He could, for example, say 'fuck' – all in the name of art – a rather revolutionary approach at the time. However, he has mixed feelings about its use nowadays: 'Certain people have a gift for saying it well.

I'm not sure whether it is a good thing or a bad thing that people say it in public more now; I imagine it is probably best kept for certain occasions. Writers who are brilliant know how much more powerful – and often how much more comic – the f-word is, if it is used sparingly. It can be deeply satisfying, especially if you are the one saying it on stage.'

Of course, with Bill it was not all work and no play. Liverpool was a bustling, vibrant place with much to offer a band of actors with a determination to live life to the full. They were allowed into clubs free, meaning as soon as their evening performance was over, they would hit the bars. Bill threw himself into this with as much enthusiasm as he had for acting: 'They were wild days. Pete [Postlethwaite] says, "Those were the days we used to work nights!"'

He was, one observer remarked, 'dangerously good at drinking'. A regular at one particular bar, he only had to reach the top of the steps leading down to the dance floor for the DJ to announce his arrival with Marvin Gaye's *Let's Get It On*. He admits that despite his true qualms about being anybody at all, this made him feel like a real star.

It was in Liverpool that he first heard Dylan's *Blood on the Tracks* album, released by Columbia records in January 1975. He bought it the day it came out, went into his room and stayed there for two weeks, putting the record on again and again, barely letting the stylus reach the end of the last track before lifting it up and going right back to side one: 'I couldn't get over it, couldn't recover from it. It's thrilling! I'd read in the paper that this genius folk singer Bob Dylan left London after a successful engagement at the 100 Club. I don't think I'd ever seen the word "genius" written down before. And it was also largely that it came before the words "folk singer."'

During his time at the Everyman, Bill met actor and writer Ken Campbell, a rather avant-garde creator, who rewrote Macbeth in pidgin English 'to make it better.' Married to actress Prunella Gee, Campbell was charismatic and entertaining; he made his mark on Bill. Together with fellow actor Chris Langham, he formed the Science Fiction Theatre of Liverpool and set about adapting the *Illuminatus!* Trilogy – a mix of sex, drugs and mythology written by Robert Anton Wilson and Robert Shea. Campbell turned the trilogy into five plays, recruited Bill, Prunella Gee, Langham and David Rappaport and set the opening date for 23 November 1976. It was a significant date, for Campbell had each play comprising five 23-minute acts because the number 23 is given a mystical significance in the books. But the project appeared to be cursed: five members of the cast were injured in accidents in the run-up to the show. Bill was one of them. He was in a serious car crash with a girlfriend and fractured his thigh, which meant he was out of the Liverpool run of *Illuminatus!* He did make it onto the stage for the London run at the National Theatre, though.

It was then such early days for Bill and his acting career. 'I had a very tortuous professional life in my younger days. I spent a lot of time on stages properly ashamed of myself, and it took me a long time to feel any pride around my job.' In 2005, he told the *Scotsman* that he was always considering giving the whole thing up: 'If anyone asked what I did for a living, I never said "actor" because as far as I was concerned, I wasn't one. I used to hitchhike up and down the country – in those days you could – and if I was going to Nottingham or Liverpool for a play, I'd tell people I was the stage electrician or something. I would never tell anyone I was going to work in a theatre because I never felt good in my mouth to say, "Well, I'm an actor." I didn't believe it. It probably took me longer than most people to put my name and the word "actor" in the same sentence. That kind of led on.

'Obviously I got over that. Acting for me then was scary and horrible, and I always thought I'd give up after the next job and get round to what I really wanted to do. What young people did then was buy a VW Microbus and paint it purple and head for Afghanistan, but I wouldn't have made it to Dover. I have a notorious reputation with motorised transport – I'm always crashing into things. And me a garage-owner's son, too.'

Bill also had the temptations of some of his friends to content with from time to time. They provided him with excuses not to work – and drugs to smoke while he thought about it, recalls Bill: 'We used to expand our consciousness on a regular basis, and they'd sit me down and go: "Bill, man, you've got to stop this shit, 'cause these middle-class fuck-pigs, these straights will fuck you up." And I'd say: "Boys, I've got to make a living," and they'd say: "We can make money, sell some hash, you know. Bill, you want to talk about theatre? The Stones is theatre, man. You want acting? Walking through customs with a couple of kilos – that's acting."'

The late 1970s saw Bill appear on television for the first time. Later, he accepted such jobs simply because he had a family and a mortgage to pay. Then he appeared in the police series, *Softly, Softly*, playing Albert Blake, a bank robber. It was the last of his son's performances that Alfred Nighy saw, as he died in 1976. Poignantly, it was one that prompted him to encourage his son to stick with acting.

Bill was later to recall: 'After scaling the dizzy heights of Bank Robber No. 3 in *Softly, Softly*, I was giving it all up again. Dad said, "You must be doing something right, keep going." He talked me round. He never said, but I think he was quite proud of me. And like everyone who's lost a parent early, I'm sad he's not still here because I think he would have got such a bang out of what I'm doing now.' For him, his father's death was the end of 'a rare and remarkable man who remains the major influence in my life. One of the first things that occurs to me when I think of any success that I have had is that I wish my dad was alive. My mother got an opportunity to see some of the good things that happened to me professionally, but my father never did. I would have liked it. It would have been the one thing he could have enjoyed; he deserved it. It would have given him enormous pride.'

His affection for his father is obvious. He thanks him for teaching him to be well mannered and courteous: 'He was also determinedly honest, almost to the point of eccentricity. And he taught me never to hold a grudge. He said, "You deal with it and once it's done, you get on with it."'

But what would Mr Nighy senior have thought of Bill's debut big screen venture? It was the rather salacious 1979 film *The Bitch*, starring Joan Collins. Bill played a delivery boy, but his scene hit the cutting-room floor and was absent from the final film.

In November 1978, he was back with his pals Julie Walters and Bernard Hill in *Soldiers Talking Cleanly*, a Play for Today by Mike Scott. He played a man called Bill. This was followed by another Scott play, *Comings and Goings*, which was to show that swearing when performing was the least of his concerns: this time, Bill had a nude scene. 'That was even worse,' he recalls, of his role as Vernon Crouch. 'The deep winter in the Hampstead Theatre Club, which had no central heating, and I was supposed to come on as if emerging from a shower. One of the female stagehands had to pour a bucket of water over me just before I came on and the water was always ice-cold. What there was of my manhood would retreat into my torso. In the matinée, you could hear the audience talking and one day I distinctly heard a woman say: "Oh no, that's disgusting!"'

But he did not want to protest because 'they would have told me I was being paranoid. Too right, I'm paranoid! I've nothing on and there are 200 people staring at me.' The thought of baring all always filled him with dread. Wherever possible, he avoided sex scenes because he was 'too shy' and because his 'difficult body' meant he didn't want to show it off 'as I knew that when it got around I was dead in the water and if a future Mrs Nighy was out there, I would be single for the rest of my life.'

His next performance was as Gorman in *Illuminations* at the Lyric Theatre, Hammersmith. This was the first play by political journalist Peter Jenkins and also starred Paul Eddington, Nigel Stock and Judy Loe.

Television was extending Bill a sort of welcome too. In 1979, he played the minor roles of a 'young man' in the TV film *Death Watch* and 'Nick' in *Fat*. Then, in December of that year, he took on the title role in a TV film *Deasey*. Though they weren't significant parts, TV did help the slightly struggling actor out in other ways. Bill recalls: 'I used to get cheap clothes off the jobs I had on the telly. It was usually a suit and that was all I had.'

In his early days, he was living in what really equated to squats, sometimes with fellow actors, but more often on his own. And the only other additions to his wardrobe were one pair of socks and a pair of Doc Martens: 'After 18 months you had to put them out on the window sill if anyone came over and you got lucky...'

Chapter Three

The Trouble With Shakespeare

1980 was a good year for Bill. His relationship with David Hare meant great changes in his life, professionally and personally. When Sir David was asked by the National Theatre's artistic director, Peter Hall, to form a company of actors, Bill became a founding member of the ensemble, which also included Anthony Hopkins.

In January he was cast in *Dreams of Leaving*, a BBC film directed and written by Hare. In it, he played William, an ambitious young journalist from Nottingham, whose marriage is falling apart and who is trying to make his mark on Fleet Street aided by an established hack, played by Mel Smith. Bill's character falls for a beautiful art gallery assistant (Kate Nelligan). As she descends into madness, he descends into cynicism about his job. This was a very powerful production, with a fine performance from Bill.

Director Richard Eyre, later to direct Nighy in other projects, recalls: 'I remember thinking how unusual Bill was because he was undemonstrative when other actors of his generation were all after burning holes in the screen or on the stage. Bill was so much more diffident, and I think a lot of people kind of took him on that level and thought that diffidence was not a virtue, whereas I always thought that it was a fantastically powerful and unusual position.'

Also in 1980, Bill appeared in BBC2's 'Playhouse' version of Malcolm Bradbury's *Standing in for Henry* and with Maureen Lipman in the TV sit-com *Agony*. Lipman played a magazine agony aunt with her own problems, including a wayward husband (Simon Williams). Bill thoroughly enjoyed a bit of scene stealing in seven episodes as Vincent Fish, a sex-mad hack, who makes erotic films on the side. He might not have made a journalist in real life, but he was certainly making up for it on screen.

Things were looking up for the actor, although he would still be well into middle age before he hit the big time. Certainly, he was bemused to find he was working: 'I wasn't drawn to act. I thought, "in a minute I'll give it up and get round to what I'm supposed to be doing" – but I never worked that out and I'm a procrastinator of the highest order. So they kept giving me jobs and I went from job to job. They used to say, "You must be prepared for long periods of unemployment," and whenever anyone said that, I'd quietly exult because this was what I had in mind.

The idea that you could legitimately loaf was glamorous for me.'

In 1981, he was back with Kate Nelligan in *Eye of the Needle*, Ken Follett's World War Two thriller, with Donald Sutherland as a German spy on a remote English island trying to get details of the D-Day landings. Bill made a brief appearance as Blenkinsop, a squadron leader. It was yet another early part that barely lists him among the credits.

A more rewarding project was a BBC radio adaptation of *The Lord of the Rings* in which, credited as William Nighy, he played Samwise Gamgee to Ian Holme's Frodo. Michael Hordern also starred. Broadcast in 13 episodes over 26 weeks, the production won great acclaim. Some 20 years later, copies were given to all the cast members by Peter Jackson when he made his film series, prompting Bill to comment: 'Someone told me Peter Jackson distributed copies of the radio version to the cast and crew. And since I get 0.00001% in royalties every time someone buys the CD, I've been getting £40 instead of £20 over the last couple of years!' He wasn't really complaining, seeing how he had to admit that the radio series, 'made me more money than I had ever had in my life.' *The Lord of the Rings* heralded a regular radio stint for Bill, including *Yes, Minister*, when he teamed up once again with his *Illuminations* co-star Paul Eddington.

In 1982, he turned down a role in *Coronation Street* (much to his mother's horror) and admitted that telling her that he had been offered a part in Britain's longest-running soap was 'a big mistake.' Bill was next seen on TV in another 'Play for Today', this time *Under the Skin*, written by *Coronation Street* writer Janey Preger and about tensions in the women's movement. He played 'Dave' and his co stars were Frances Tomelty and Jacqueline Tong. Following this, he appeared in a 'Play for Tomorrow' called *Easter 2016*, made by BBC Northern Ireland and written by Graham Reid. The play centred around Northern Ireland's only mixed-religion teacher training college, where Bill's character, charismatic teacher Connor Mullan, goes against the demands of a bullying security force and tries to involve the students in a centenary re-enactment of the Easter rising.

In 1983, Bill appeared in 'Model Murder', an episode of *Jemima Shore Investigates*, with Patricia Hodge. There was another fleeting appearance as an Ear, Nose and Throat doctor in *Curse of the Pink Panther*, plus as a 'baddie' German called Goschen in an episode of *Reilly: Ace of Spies* called *The Visiting Fireman*, with Reilly (Sam Neill) battling for the British in World War One and being asked to infiltrate a German armaments plant.

Better things were on the horizon for Bill's acting and personal life, though. He appeared as Stephen Andrews in the National's *Map of the World*, set in a lavish Bombay hotel in 1978, with a UNESCO conference on world poverty taking place nearby. The production also starred a certain British actress called

Diana Quick. One of four children and the daughter of a dentist, the actress first trained at the National Youth Theatre and then, aged 17, went on to study English Literature at Oxford. She was also the first female president of the Oxford University Drama Society.

During her time there, she was part of *The Oxford Line*, a comedy revue with John Sergeant, Simon Brett and Nigel Rees. It was while she was at Oxford that 19-year-old Diana learned of her beloved father's death by finding an urgent note in her student pigeonhole. She later recalled in the *Guardian* that the following events were a blur as she travelled to the family home near Dartford to see her mother Joan, older sister Julie and brothers Clive and Robert. Together, they visited the body of Leonard Quick, the man Diana described as 'warm, gregarious and sociable.'

Until then, she had lived a charmed and happy life and she was devastated by her father's death. The almost arrogant confidence she once had disappeared, never to return: 'You don't consider it, do you? You feel immortal and you feel those about you are. Very few people I knew had died, I didn't really think about getting old and dying. He was 50. From where I am now, that seems cruelly young.'

Quick had turned down a place at RADA 'because I had been a student for five years' and instead undertook voice training with the late Kate Fleming of the National Theatre. Her stage appearances included two Edward Bond plays: *Lear* and *The Sea* at the Royal Court and Ridley Scott's debut *The Duellists*. By the time she met Bill she had been nominated for both Emmy and BAFTA awards for her role as Lady Julia Flyte in television's mini-series *Brideshead Revisited*, the year before, playing alongside such luminaries as Sir John Gielgud, Sir Laurence Olivier, Anthony Andrews and Jeremy Irons. That had all happened despite protests from her mother that she would never make it as an actress.

'She suggested I do anything with a regular wage packet and we used to really fight about it. In the end I said, "Just leave me alone till I'm 25 and if I'm not making a living, I'll reconsider." By 23, I was playing a lead in *Billy Liar* at Drury Lane with Michael Crawford and Elaine Paige and she was bringing a coach-load to see me.'

Diana had enjoyed a seven-year relationship with Albert Finney, whose professional advice to her included, 'You're going to find it very hard to have a career in England. The English don't really like grown-up women – they only like girls.' Previously she was married to the actor Kenneth Cranham, who she met while with the National Youth Theatre. Diana unwittingly shared one of Bill's passions. She was once invited back to Cranham's house to listen to a Bob Dylan album. 'I thought he was great,' she recalls. Whether the two talked of this common interest when they first met, we will never know, but Bill certainly felt a strong attraction for the actress, who in 1984 was described as one of the 'most beautiful women in the world.'

Bill recalls, 'I first spotted Diana on the front cover

of a magazine with the headline: IS THIS THE MOST BEAUTIFUL WOMAN IN THE WORLD? I didn't know whether she was, but I did know she was extremely beautiful. In *Map of the World* I was supposed to play a man who was in pretty good shape, apart from the fact that he had difficulty breathing when a certain woman walked into the room. That woman was played by Diana. It was an example of life reflecting art, in my case. I was struck by her instantly, though I don't suppose for one moment that it was love at first sight for her.'

Despite their widely differing backgrounds – though both attended grammar school, Diana was the one to pass exams – one thing the two had in common besides acting and a love of Bob Dylan, was their star sign of Sagittarius. Diana was born on 23 November 1946, making her just over three years older than Bill. Eventually, the two got together and would become, in all senses of the word, man and wife – except they would never marry. Bill said he once proposed to Diana, but her reply was, 'No – and don't ask me again.' Throughout their relationship, though, they would refer to each other as 'husband and wife' because it made things less 'difficult'. Also, said Bill, 'I am never happy with any of the alternatives.' It wasn't long before the pair realised they *did* have a few other traits in common – both admit their worst fault is procrastination and both, many years later, would bitterly regret their smoking habits.

In April that year Bill appeared as Colin Street in two

episodes of a TV series called *Fox*, in which Peter Vaughan was an East End godfather and Ray Winstone and Bernard Hill played two of his sons. After this came a TV film debut in a new adaptation of *Little Lord Fauntleroy*, directed by Jack Gold, who had just scored a hit with Richard Burton in *The Midas Touch*. Co-stars included Alec Guinness, Eric Porter and a young Patrick Stewart. Bill's role was 'Officer'.

In the mid-eighties, Bill's screen career enjoyed a gentle ascent. He played the part of Al in a feature film of John le Carré's *The Little Drummer Girl* in 1984. Directed by George Hill, Diane Keaton starred as an American actress called Charley, recruited by Israeli intelligence to ensnare terrorists. David Suchet and Anna Massey also appeared. Bill was well down the cast list, but it wasn't a bad early project. That same year, he appeared in an episode of the daytime TV series *Crown Court*, playing a character called Lee Sinclair. It wasn't his most satisfying of acting years, but 1984 brought him a very special joy which would more than compensate: Diana gave birth to their daughter on 17 July.

It wasn't just two names that the girl would have to live up to when she much later followed in her parents' acting footsteps. She was named Mary Bing Jamie Alfreda Leonora Quick Kit Nighy. Diana was 37 when she gave birth to Mary and, like countless other women, suffered the conflict between career and motherhood: 'When I was younger, I thought I had all the time in the world to have children and all I really wanted to do was work, but I had quite a lot of pressure put on me by our family doctor, who was also a friend. When I went to him for advice about birth control, he would continually ask when I was going to start having babies. I would say I didn't want them now and wasn't it better to have them when I wanted to, and wouldn't resent them? He said it was better, physically, to have them when you are young and I think he was, up to a point, correct.'

But Diana knew that once a baby arrived, it would complete the happiness for her and Bill. She said: 'I'd been married before I met him and had other important relationships, but until Bill I had never thought that I wanted to have a child. When Mary arrived I felt a mixture of emotions, including panic and overwhelming love. I felt a great sense of responsibility, not just towards my child, but also towards her father.'

But there would be no more children for Bill and Diana and this was the cause of some regret, with Diana saying: 'I was physically well when I had Mary, but I didn't have any more children. It would have been nice for her to have had a brother or sister, but it just didn't happen, so perhaps I should have started a family younger.'

In 1985, Bill had a role in a four-part TV series called *The Last Place on Earth*, directed by Ferdinand Fairfax, in which Martin Shaw (one of TV's car-crashing, all-action *Professionals*) played Robert Falcon Scott, preparing for his South Pole expedition.

Bill was dog-handler Cecil Meares. Also in the series was a very young Hugh Grant.

Following this was another well-received television drama, *Hitler's SS: Portrait in Evil*. The two-part drama focussed on two brothers: Bill as Helmut Hoffman, a brilliant student and self-styled opportunist, who joins Hitler's SS and his younger brother Karl – played by John Shea – a top athlete who becomes a chauffeur for Hitler's storm troopers, the SA. When the SS topples the SA from power, Karl ends up in Dachau. He is 'rescued' through his brother's influence, though he ends up on the Russian Front. As he watches the Third Reich deteriorate, at long last Helmut suffers pangs of conscience. Interwoven in the grim tale is a love triangle between Helmut, Karl and a beautiful nightclub singer Mitzi Templer, played by Lucy Gutteridge.

The supporting cast included Carroll Baker as the Hoffman brothers' anguished mother, Tony Randall as an androgynous entertainer named Putzi and David Warner, repeating his Holocaust role as SS head man Heydrich. Bill's involvement in *Hitler's SS* also saw him reunited with *Softly, Softly* co-star Stratford Johns, who played a bartender, and John Normington (Himmler), who had appeared in *Comings and Goings*. A young Warren Clarke and Michael Elphick played SS and SAS officers respectively.

The year ended with *Thirteen at Dinner*, an Agatha Christie TV adaptation starring Peter Ustinov (the original Inspector Poirot) and David Suchet, (the future Poirot). The plot involved the death of one Lord Edgware, fatally wounded with a knife to the back of his head. Bill played Rodney March, his unscrupulous nephew, who inherits all his money.

That same year Bill enjoyed theatre success when he teamed up again with David Hare for *Pravda* at the Olivier Theatre. Hare co-wrote the play with Howard Brenton, author of the controversial *Romans in Britain*. Anthony Hopkins took the lead as Lambert Le Roux, a Robert Maxwell-style newspaper magnate. Bill played Le Roux's Australian business manager, Eaton Sylvester. The role had him swotting up on an Australian accent: 'I went to the place to find Australians in London, which I was told is the Chelsea Arts Club. So I went directly to the Chelsea Arts Club with my tape recorder and my script. And I had a very, very, very good time. I went in the bar there and I put the tape recorder on the bar; I put the script next to it and I bought them all drinks, and in exchange for them reading the script into the tape recorder, I had some hysterical tapes, I must say. Very funny.'

But for Bill, appearing on stage brought with it all the usual anxieties. It was another opening, another show. Would it be OK?

'I was standing behind the flat, a part of the stage, with Anthony Hopkins in the dark and we couldn't actually see each other. He asked me how I felt. It was the first night and I said, "I'm shitting myself" and he said, "So am I. It gets worse..." I thought if he's shitting himself, then we are buggered. And he went on and brought the house to its knees. I have never seen anyone act better than Sir Anthony Hopkins in that play. It was a powerful part; he was scary as hell.'

Bill was to work once more with Hare and Hopkins in the much-acclaimed 1986 production of *King Lear*, again at the Olivier. To a backdrop of flashing lights and white sails, Hopkins let rip with his tormented Lear. Meanwhile, Bill gave an amazing performance as Edgar, cast out and pretending to be as insane as 'poor Tom', protecting his father and beating his evil brother Edmund in a fight. But he took early retirement from Shakespeare: 'There are those who would point out that, for an actor, performing Shakespeare is a challenge, but that holds no appeal. For generations, when people have been asked to do Shakespeare, they bend one leg, put their other hand on their sword, put their chin up slightly and start talking funny.

'It is like it is handed down in the DNA, it is really bizarre. It is to be resisted because it is not good for anybody and it is not good for business. I've never been one for challenges, I've been challenged enough – just getting up in the morning is a challenge. I quietly retired from Shakespeare in my bathroom so that I don't have to think about it any more. I thought I would put myself out of my misery. That way, when they come on the phone and say, "Would you like to play...?" I've already made my decision and I don't have to worry about it anymore.

'I was pleased to be involved in the two Shakespeare

plays I have done, but other than that I don't really have much experience of Shakespeare and I don't really have much enthusiasm for investigating the performing of it. I am very happy to let other people do it. There is nothing lonelier than being on stage in pantaloons. I used to joke that I can't operate in those kind of trousers, but actually it's not a joke – I really can't. I can only really operate in a decent lounge suit. Have you ever stood in a pair of trousers that stop at the knees and a pair of stockings? I'm not working in an anorak, I'm not working in tights and I particularly don't want to be armed. I am aware Shakespeare is the greatest poet the world has ever known, but the performing of it is something I'd rather leave to others.'

The next year brought more stage success in *Mean Tears*, at the Cottesloe Theatre. Written and directed by Peter Gill, the play explored sexuality, with Bill as Julian, a bisexual. He might not have been seen on television in 1987, but he was still heard: Bill provided the voice of Judge Gilbert in the TV series *Muzzy*.

It was when daughter Mary was two and a half years old that he felt that the happy world with which he had been blessed was about to be shattered. Diana Quick was driving her car when she and Mary were involved in a crash. Their daughter was badly injured and forced to undergo six hours of surgery. 'Because I was driving, I felt absolutely wretched,' Diana later recalled. 'I re-ran it in my mind, wondering if there was anything I could have done differently to save us, but it was a monster pile-up in fog and we went straight into the tail-gate of a lorry. Mary suffered serious internal injuries because of the impact against the seatbelt. All my energy went into willing her to survive and thankfully, she did.'

The theatre kept Bill from both film and TV screens until 1989, when he appeared as opera house manager Martin Barton in the feature film of Gaston Leroux's *The Phantom of the Opera*. Robert 'Freddy' Englund played the phantom; Stephanie Lawrence was La Carlotta while Jill Schoelen was Christine Day.

There was also a cameo role in a TV series called *South of the Border*, in which Bill played a character called Tony Freeson.

His first appearance of the 1990s was as Sam Courtney in a TV series, *Making News*. The part called for Bill to once again join the world of newspapers. Co-stars were Celia Imrie, Paul Darrow (the moody Avon in *Blake's Seven*) and Richard Attenborough's daughter, Charlotte. That same year he was in *Mack the Knife*, an ambitious adaptation of Bertolt Brecht and Kurt Weill's *The Threepenny Opera*. It was a musical/opera in which Bill played Tiger Brown, police chief and best friend of Mack. The role called for him to sport a beard and to dance and sing. There was also a Scottish accent – to be resurrected many years later for evil squid Davy Jones.

The plot revolved around London's underground world with gang boss Mackie Messer falling in love with the beautiful Polly, daughter of beggar king Peachum, and planning to marry her. The wedding is set to take place in a warehouse, decorated for the nuptials with goods stolen from London's finest shops and attended by a ragbag of villains and thieves. Peachum strongly opposes the marriage, though. He puts pressure on Tiger Brown to send Mackie to the gallows, threatening to organise a beggars' revolt to disrupt the Queen's upcoming Coronation if the police chief does not accede to his wishes. Richard Harris played the crime boss and Bill's friend Julie Walters was his wife.

There was also an appearance in a TV film called *Writing on the Wall*, playing a character called Brill. His next TV piece was the black comedy *Absolute Hell*, which aired on 5 October 1991. Shot on video as part of the BBC's excellent 'Performance' strand, a classy little sepia opener leads into colour. Judi Dench plays club owner Christine, but the real honours (as one reviewer said) went to Bill as homosexual novelist Hugh Marriner, heavily in debt and experiencing relationship difficulties.

The story was set in a Soho drinking club amid a bomb-devastated London in the weeks leading up to the 1945 general election. *Absolute Hell* grew out of Rodney Ackland's 1952 play *The Pink Room* (also known as *The Escapists*), which had been a major flop. Ackland himself felt it was too watered down and in the 1980s he reworked and re-titled it, turning it into a real gem. Directed by Anthony Page, *Absolute Hell* also starred Francesca Annis and Bill's *Fox* co-star, Ray Winstone. Bill remembers one particular scene with Judi Dench with delight: 'A chap comes in with a gun and says, "Who wants a bullet up the botty?" Judi just looked at me with the most unprofessional look anyone has ever given me and we never got through that scene without corpsing.' Corpsing or not, he did the part proud with one critic enthusing, 'but the real honours go to Bill Nighy yet again...'

That year, he returned to the stage in Harold Pinter's *Betrayal* at the Almeida, featuring Cheryl Campbell and *Last Place on Earth* co-star Martin Shaw. In a bitter autobiographical tale of Pinter's affair with broadcaster Joan Bakewell, he plays Pinter, who is 'betrayed' when he discovers his lover's husband has known about the affair all along.

His next film appearance of 1991 was in the comedy *Antonia and Jane*, co-starring Imelda Staunton and Saskia Reeves. The quirky drama was produced for British television and released theatrically. Reeves played Antonia and Staunton was Jane. The two characters are long-time friends who meet up once a year to discuss how their lives are going – with each wishing they had the life of the other. They have a rather uncomfortable relationship, particularly when Jane falls for an artist – Bill – whom she meets at his exhibition of naked bottoms. Antonia steals him away, only to regret it.

Much harder-hitting was the TV series *The Men's Room*. Directed by Antonia Bird, the five-part drama follows the life of Professor Mark Carleton (Bill), head of a university department, and Charity (played by Harriet Walter), who falls in love with him. Both are married, but while Charity has a conscience about her infidelity, Carleton is a serial philanderer. He needs to have affairs, he tells Charity, because they keep him 'vital'. Their relationship turns into a rollercoaster, where they can't seem to live with or without each other. The story ends in the year 2000, twenty years after their initial meeting. They are now living separate lives, but even so many years later, there still seems to be a spark of passion between the two. It was pretty raunchy stuff and Bill recalls, 'There was a period when women felt they couldn't relax around me, up the shops. It soon wore off!'

There were also small roles in some of television's most popular series of the time. Bill played a character called Steve Reeves, a DJ with a penchant for under-age girls, in an episode of *Boon* and Barry, a character in a Christmas 'special' of the Channel Islands cop series, *Bergerac*.

1992 was another year in which he enjoyed a challenging time on stage and screen. That year saw Bill reunited with Antonia Bird and Imelda Staunton in *A Masculine Ending*, based on a Joan Smith novel in which a feminist academic played by Janet McTeer, suspects her college colleagues of murder. Bill played her ex-husband – and a journalist yet again!

Next came an episode of *Chillers*, based on a short story by Patricia Highsmith called 'Something the Cat Dragged In', in which Bill played a character called Tom Dickinson and starred opposite Edward Fox and Michael Hordern.

1993 was a busier year. Bill's 'clean' image now had the parts coming in thick and fast. He appeared in the children's fantasy series, *Eye of the Storm* – claimed to be one of the scariest TV shows ever produced for kids.

Bill played environmentalist Tom Frewen, father of a teenage daughter. The two must prevent the evil Judy Parfitt from causing an almighty eco-disaster.

His next role was as Julian in Bill Forsyth's *Being Human* with Robin Williams, followed by *Unnatural Causes*, part of the 'Murder!' series and based on P. D. James' novel. Adam Dalgliesh investigates the murder of a writer on the Suffolk coast. Bill plays a critic, Oliver Latham, who has panned the dead man's final play.

After another cameo as Alan Sinclair in the country doctor series, *Peak Practice*, Bill appeared as John Tracey in *Don't Leave Me This Way*, a follow-up to *A Masculine Ending*, with Janet McTeer and Imelda Staunton recreating their roles as amateur sleuths investigating the death of a friend in a car crash.

There was also a TV presentation of Ronald Mackenzie's popular play, *The Maitlands*, set in the secluded coastal resort of Betworthy, where the Maitland family has fallen on hard times. Bill plays the eldest son Roger, a schoolmaster forced to give a young boy after-hours tuition in order to pay for his jet-setting wife Dorothy's trip to the French Riviera. Edward Fox, Eileen Atkins, Jennifer Ehle, Emma Fielding and Harriet Walter also starred.

Bill's biggest success of 1993 was on stage, reunited with Emma Fielding and Harriet Walter in Tom Stoppard's *Arcadia* at the Lyttleton Theatre. Directed by Trevor Nunn, *Arcadia* opened on 13 April and had Bill playing the role of Bernard Nightingale opposite Felicity Kendal's rival academic, Hannah Jarvis.

He also appeared as the opportunist novelist Trigorin

in a modern adaptation of Anton Chekov's *The Seagull* at the Olivier Theatre. This gave him the rather embarrassing opportunity of cavorting with Judi Dench on a rug, as she played the ageing actress Arkadina. Later, he revealed that working so closely with Dench and in such a project had been career changing: 'That was a revelation to me – I'd heard other actors say how marvellous Chekov was, but I didn't really understand until I came to do it. It is a bit like a blank cheque in as much as he is deeply sophisticated in so much as you are at liberty to draw your character as you might wish. Obviously there are constraints, but it's a very open kind of way of working.

'It was a big deal for me, that particular production. I had a kind of revelation doing it in that I realised there is a line between the wings and the stage and I was rather pathetically at my then time of life, kind of crossing that line. And when I crossed it, because I was in front of people, I was suddenly on my best behaviour in some way. I would stand differently and because I was in period clothing, I would arrange my body in a different way. You think, hang on! People didn't stand any differently in those days – they stood badly, like everybody else. And I would suddenly start not doing things and editing my movement, and also speaking rather well. It was all not to any great purpose and it wasn't helping, so I did experiment with just crossing the line and having nothing change. Other people probably came to this conclusion years ago, but it took me a while. It was very big and important in my experience; it was another brick out of the wall of what they call naturalism.'

But nothing, absolutely nothing, would change his anxieties about coupling on stage or screen: 'Everything that has to do with pretending to make love to a woman, it's deeply, deeply embarrassing, because you do it in a room full of people. Lots of men, lots of women... And you have to have your bum made up – that's a really embarrassing moment – and you have to simulate passion with noises, and you never know what noises other people make, so it's quite embarrassing.'

Chapter Four

A Stage Further

Bill credits his long-time agent, Pippa Markham, for spotting early on that he'd be more successfully employed in character roles than in those where he'd have to take himself too seriously: 'I've never been able to take myself seriously as an object of desire or love. If I have difficulty in any area, that's the area where I have conceded.'

But his regular stage appearances did cut him off from the 'real world'. For around ten years, when he was putting his heart and soul into up to eight shows a week, he watched no TV and listened to no radio, 'because theatre was my thing.' Nor did he spend evenings agonising over what actors call their 'process' when playing a part: 'I used to sit in digs late at night after we'd played Monopoly and had a few drinks and people would talk about their "process". I didn't know what they were talking about. I would keep schtum and not contribute to that part of the conversation and hope that nobody asked me anything because I didn't have a process; I just used to make it up as I went along. I wish I had a process, but now it is too late. I put in some hours, but I do it largely off the top of my head. As a younger actor I didn't have a method, that was my dirty secret.'

In fact, his only on-screen appearances of 1994 were in an episode of *Wycliffe*, in which he played David Cleeve, a novelist living in a large house in Cornwall (the character receives playing cards through the post and after the receipt of each card, there is a death) and a TV mini-series titled *God's Messengers*.

Bill's next television opportunity came in 1996 when, although he wasn't actually seen, he lent his voice to Jonathan Myerson's animated bible stories, *Testament*, playing Belshazzar, the Babylonian king who worshipped gold, disrespected God and subsequently received his comeuppance. Following this, he appeared as Tristan in Martin Sherman's *Indian Summer* (also known as *Alive and Kicking*), which brought about a reunion with Everyman friend Antony Sher. It recounted the story of a ballet dancer with AIDS (played by Jason Flemyng) as he prepared for his biggest role.

He then played Jeremy Saville in *True Blue*, featuring Tom Hollander and directed by Ferdinand Fairfax. The film told the true story of the Oxford Boat Race Mutiny of 1987. Although Bill was not singularly picked out, he had the satisfaction of being among a cast which overall won good reviews. Said one critic,

Rachel Quarrell: 'This is the rowing film from Britain, certainly of the century, probably of all time. *True Blue* is competently filmed, pacey and interesting; the acting is strong, and the film works for several levels.

'Ferdinand Fairfax's film, full of fine performances, builds the tension through a series of confrontations and a constantly shifting balance of power over the year leading up to the race. The intuitive relationship between the besieged Topolski (the excellent Johan Leysen) and the President of the College Captains, Donald McDonald (the quietly impassioned Dominic West), is particularly well drawn. With more than a hint of *Chariots of Fire*, not least in the Vangelis-like soundtrack, this is a moving and beautifully observed film about sporting passion'.

Though his output was prolific, Bill remained in the frustrating situation of being cast in cameo roles. In 1997 he appeared in an episode of the TV series *Kavanagh QC* as Giles Culpepper QC and was the voice of Long John Silver in an animated film version of *Treasure Island*. He also played Edward Gardner, assistant to Sir Arthur Conan Doyle (Peter O'Toole) in *FairyTale: A True Story*, which was based on two young English cousins, Florence Hoath (Elsie Wright) and Elizabeth Earl (Frances Griffiths), who said they had discovered and photographed fairies.

1997 also saw him back with David Hare, this time at the Vaudeville for *Skylight*, in which Bill played Tom Sergeant, a widowed restaurateur who takes up with an ex-mistress. Directed by Richard Eyre, the play had been a success on opening two years earlier when Michael Gambon took the lead, but critics said Bill went on to make the part his own. Indeed, well before he was offered the role himself, he was congratulating Gambon on his appearance.

Little knowing that he would ever be cast in the work himself, Bill was knocked out after watching it as a member of the audience: 'I hardly ever write to anyone but I wrote to Sir Michael and I wrote to Sir Richard and I telephoned Sir David [Hare was knighted in 1998] and I said to all of them, "Thank you all very, very much." It's like when you're a kid and you go to Saturday morning pictures to see *Zorro* or *Jetman* and you would swordfight all the way home or be Jetman in the air because it was all so exciting. Coming out of *Skylight* was like that for me. I didn't swordfight, but I did dance all the way home. The idea that you did the same job as them and involved in the same kind of endeavour as they are, made you proud to be part of it. Their acting was of the highest order.'

He was both excited and anxious when he took the call from David Hare to appear in *Skylight*: 'The original was such a beautiful thing and when the revival came around and they called me, I thought, "I can't do that. It's beyond my capabilities." And then David calls and I hear his voice and I say, "I'll do it!"'

Ever independent when it comes to tackling a new role, as soon as he was cast in the play, Bill called Richard Eyre and asked if he could learn his lines ahead of rehearsal time. This, apparently, is not what most actors do. 'It's a very odd phenomenon that I should have felt compelled to make that call because there was a kind of piece of nonsense in my view that entered the language, which was that to learn one's lines before you got to rehearsal for a theatre play was a discourtesy to your fellow professionals because you would learn intonations you would then become imprisoned by, and therefore you were not at liberty to work with them in a free and natural manner. It is actually scoundrel talk of the highest order. It makes no sense... it just means you left the script in the bar or something. But it was a very big taboo and it entered the language in a big way. It's like when you are on camera, do nothing. That's another piece of nonsense. Check my early work and you'll see a young man doing absolutely nothing. It was boring...'

Skylight was to earn him one of his early awards – a Barclays Theatre Award, presented by the Theatrical Management Association, for Best Actor. *Skylight* went on to become one of Bill's personal favourites. He described it as, 'one of the most exciting and inspirational plays I've ever read or been in. I'll bet my house that it will be performed a hundred years from now. It's a great work. It delivers what it intends to say while thoroughly involving you with the characters and the situation. It's successful on every level and also very satisfying because it's funny. It is a great work.'

He also praised Hare's *Arcadia* and *Betrayal*: 'They are touched by genius, that is no reference to me. The plays are as if direct from God, if there is one... Works of art and deeply entertaining.'

Next came another Harold Pinter work, *A Kind of Alaska*, staged at the Donmar Warehouse and directed by Karel Reisz (who made his name with Alan Sillitoe's *Saturday Night and Sunday Morning* and then later with *The French Lieutenant's Woman*). Bill plays Dr Hornby, who is trying to reassure a teenager trapped in a decaying body.

When *Still Crazy* came along in 1998 it was as if he was being given a dress rehearsal for the role which in five years' time would send his star status soaring. Bill plays Ray Simms, a flamboyant rock singer unable to cope with day-to-day living, but fighting shy of a return to his drink-and-drug days. The film tells the story of a keyboard player trying to re-form his seventies' glam rock band, Strange Fruit. This was a highly significant project in terms of Bill's career and he credits director Brian Gibson – who sadly died shortly afterwards – for one of his acting leaps: 'Brian went out on a limb for me. It meant everything. It's a Catch 22: you can't play the lead role in a movie until you've played the lead role in a movie. There are landmarks through your career, even though you're the only person who chronicles them privately.

'There's no question about it. Brian Gibson put me in the movies, really. I'd played one other substantial part in *FairyTale*, which wasn't a huge part... Charles Sturridge was the first person to give me a substantial role in a movie, but Brian Gibson was the first person to give me a principal role in a movie and it did make all the difference, because although the film wasn't commercially very successful – it was supposed to survive without any promotion at all, and it couldn't do that – people who have seen it, liked it... So, it set the precedent. In other words, I'd played a principal role in a movie and it was successful, so I could play principal roles in movies.

'So, that was the big turning point... And you know, you have a choice. It was a big day actually, because my agent said to me for various reasons, "You don't have to go, if you don't want to." There were technical reasons why I could have bowed out. And in the old days, I might just have said, "Yeah, you know what – forget it, I don't want to go through it." But I actually turned up. And there's a point where you think: I could leave the building now. I could just walk out, go down the street, you know, get a sandwich, or else I can just humiliate myself as a middle-aged man in front of this camera with my midriff showing. And I decided to humiliate myself. But, in fact, the confusion in my mind was that I was supposed to be some kind of plausible rock god, but of course I was supposed to be a rock idiot. I can do "rock idiot". I don't stretch to rock god, but I got a couple of laughs and I did a couple of ancient rock'n'roll, middle-aged man jokes and they laughed. It was a big day, that was a big turning point.'

The screenplay for *Still Crazy* was written by Dick Clement and Ian La Frenais and starred a great British cast, including Timothy Spall, Jimmy Nail, Phil Davis and Frances Barber, but it was Bill, in his 'warm-up' role prior to playing Billy Mack in 2003's *Love Actually*, who stole the show. His wedding speech was a killer and the scene where he attempts to walk on ice in platforms was a classic. It was a huge role for him, but it had seemed unpromising at first: 'I remember I did this lonely screen test in a disused tax office on the outskirts of London one morning at the crack of dawn in a pair of black velvet flared loon pants and a pair of green fake-crocodile 4-inch-heeled platforms, and my top was a sort of space-aged thing with swing-wing shoulders which didn't meet my trousers, and I had hair extensions and dodgy makeup. They put me in front of a microphone with a karaoke machine, and they had me perform – there was just the cameraman, Brian Gibson, and me singing *Smoke on the Water* by Deep Purple. Can you imagine? Auditioning in a disused tax office on the outskirts of London, singing *Smoke on the Water* while dressed in loon pants and platforms and shoulder pads!'

Naturally, he must have wondered what he was doing, but it worked. Though *Still Crazy* was not a huge hit, Bill was noticed and scored immediate cult status – winning the *Evening Standard* Peter Sellers' Award for Best Comedy Performance. Strange Fruit were even offered a lot of money to tour American colleges. The film gave him the chance to be in a rock band without the angst of his real-life efforts of earlier days. As he admitted: 'I did want to be a rock and roll singer like everyone else. I never got out the bedroom. When it got close to the real thing, I panicked and fled back into the theatre so it's terrific to have done this movie. It's as close as I'll get...'

Allowed to shine, he pulled it off and won an early batch of enthusiastic reviews. *CNN* gushed: 'Then there is Ray. Played by accomplished British stage actor Bill Nighy, Ray is the lead singer and the one band member still emotionally trapped in the '70s. Nighy has the aforementioned sex, drugs and rock 'n' roll carved into his facial features (can you say Keith Richards?) and his performance is stunning – you'll find yourself wondering just which '70s band he was really in. He's responsible for much of the film's humour and pathos. You'll find yourself rooting for him to succeed, along with the others, despite his inflated and ultimately frail ego.' The *Sydney Morning Herald* remarked: 'The ending will have many cheering and crying at the same time. Bill Nighy, who hasn't realised that actors are allowed off days, is typically dazzling as the replacement singer everyone hates.'

The soundtrack from *Still Crazy* was later released, with one fan proclaiming, 'Here you get a real good taste of Bill Nighy's singing talent; he is a fantastic singer... a must have. Many rock bands would wish for a lead singer like Bill Nighy...' One of the soundtrack songs, *The Flame Still Burns*, was nominated for a Golden Globe Award for Best Song in a Motion Picture.

In 1999, Bill joined Chris Langham again in an episode of Langham's spoof documentary series, *People Like Us*, playing Will Rushmore in *The Photographer*. He was, of course, an inept photographer, despite roving reporter Roy Mallard (Langham) describing his dark room as 'the confessional in the church of the photographer's science.' It could only have been his friendship with Langham that persuaded Bill into what, for him, were excruciatingly embarrassing scenes: 'Everything that has to do with pretending to make love to a woman is deeply, deeply embarrassing, because you do it in a room full of people. Lots of men, lots of women... Once again I played an older man with a younger girlfriend, and in order to make me young, she takes me out to a shop and buys me a pair of very low-slung combat trousers that come down very low on your hips, and a very big pair of trainers, very brightly coloured trainers, and when you're my age that's a very, very sad and lonely place to be. We were filming in the streets and I had to walk up and down in public, with my trousers falling down, and these very, very big and bright trainers on, and people would look at me and would pick at me, and I looked very, very sad, but I hope it was funny.'

People Like Us won the 1999/2000 Silver Rose of Montreux for Comedy.

He also appeared in TV's *Kiss Me Kate* – no, nothing to do with Shakespeare or its offshoot musical, but a BBC sitcom starring Caroline Quentin as psychotherapist Kate. The series follows her as she tries to manage her patients' lives as well as her own – particularly as she becomes the object of desire of fellow therapist Douglas Fielding (Chris Langham), but veers towards heart doctor Iain Cameron, played by Bill. *Kiss Me Kate* ran from 1998 to 2000, but Bill only made an appearance in the last series. It was written by Chris Langham and John Morton, who worked together on *People Like Us*.

Bill had another guest spot as Mr Johnson, a guest, in Rik Mayall and Adrian Edmonson's comedy *Guest House Paradiso* (1999). The two comedians played Richie Twat and Eddie Elizabeth Ndingombaba, who run the nastiest, most squalid hotel in the world and obviously do not make any money. It's not to everyone's taste and perhaps only hardened Mayall and Edmonson fans appreciate some of the dialogue:

Mr Johnson: *I merely brushed your arm!*
Richard Twat: *Well, we have already established that you're a liar, Mr Johnson.*
Mr Johnson: *Look, Mr Twat...*
Richard Twat: *It's pronounced 'Thwaite'!*
Mr Johnson: *Well, it's spelt 'Twat'.*
[pointing at Richie's name on the desk]
Mr Johnson: *T-W-A-T. Twat!*
Richard Twat: *Could you keep your voice down, please? We do have normal guests as well.*

Also starring were Fenella Fielding, Vincent Cassel, Sophia Myles and Simon Pegg – who would go on to regularly involve Bill in his own productions.

The year 2000 began with *The Magic of Vincent*, a comedy co-starring Miranda Richardson and Emilia Fox, with Bill as a hypochondriac artist. After this, Charles Sturridge called on him to appear in a television adaptation of science writer Dava Sobel's bestselling *Longitude*. Concurrent stories involving Michael Gambon, Jeremy Irons, Frank Finlay and Stephen Fry featured. Bill plays Lord Sandwich, Secretary of State and First Lord of the Admiralty. That same year, he provided the voice-over for an episode of an animated version of *The Canterbury Tales* by Jonathan Myerson (with whom he had worked on *Testament*). Bill narrated for 'The Merchant in The Journey Back', two years after he had done the same for 'The Merchant in Leaving London'. There were also a couple more episodes of *Kiss Me Kate*. They may not have been major roles, but they helped pay the bills.

Things were slowly taking off for Bill, but at times it must have been excruciating to voluntarily expose his vulnerability and insecurity on stage or in front of a camera. It seemed the cowering little boy was still in him: 'That is probably an extreme response to being asked about myself, but it is like everybody. Take biochemists or airline pilots or veterinary surgeons, there are certain misunderstandings about what their jobs are. And with actors there are certain misconceptions, such as we are extroverts and that we have a different response to standing up and being the only one allowed to talk than a regular human being. That's not true. My reaction to standing up in front of a thousand people or a camera is exactly the same as anyone else, which is basically, "Can I go home now?" because it's scary, scary in a regular way.

'Often you do find that the people who arrange to be actors do have above average difficulty in the rest of their lives. They are slightly disabled by self-consciousness and are not particularly gregarious or extrovert and yet they seek out this incredibly public job. I am, strictly speaking, deeply unsuited temperamentally to my job. The boy cowering in the corner is an equation that is quite true some of the time. I had to find ways of overcoming my self-consciousness because I was paralysed by it to some degree. It's what you have to deal with as an actor, everybody does. It's not just me. I don't know how other people are, so I can only comment on myself, but it was, I suspect, above averagely an obstacle for me so it took me a while.'

In 2001, he played a south London hairdresser, Ray Robertson, who takes on Alan Rickman's rival character of Phil Allen at a hairdressing competition in the film *Blow Dry*. Naturally, the part called for him to appear competent at hairstyling. He spent three days in a hairdressing salon in Brighouse, Yorkshire, to gain some 'work experience', commenting afterwards: 'I could probably blow dry your hair; there would be tears in your eyes by the time I'm finished, you know, but I could make it look reasonable.' And as for cutting: 'I don't think anyone is actually gonna let me loose with a pair of scissors.' Also in the cast were Natasha Richardson, Warren Clarke, Rachel Griffiths, Josh Hartnett and supermodel Heidi Klum. All won praise, with the comment that they 'could hardly be more charming or more authentic' and Bill was singled out as a 'great comic villain.'

After this, he rejoined Tom Hollander in *Lawless Heart*, which touched on the subject of homosexuality with the death of a lover. The film was written and directed by Tom Hunsinger and Neil Hunter. Bill plays married Dan, who after the death tries to grab life by the throat. One attempt involves an encounter with sexy French florist (Clémentine Célarié), who he meets at a party.

The script was devised to allow actors to improvise. Recalls Bill: 'Tom called and asked if I would go and improvise a script. Then, after explaining the story, characters and their relationships, I and the other actors sat around a kitchen table with lots of coffee, improvising scenes while Tom and Neil made lots of tapes, which were used to build up the characters.' His improvisation greatly impressed the writers, with Hunter saying that he was 'striking' with 'lots of rich and detailed ideas' and Hunsinger remarking, 'Bill was an incredibly professional and nice person to work with – he was so inventive.'

One of his character's strongest lines – 'I once faked a broken heart but ran out of energy' has been frequently quoted. Another key line, straight from the heart, was when Dan ponders how he is 'rather flattered' to be called 'depressed', adding: 'I suppose I have emotions, but I don't make a meal of them.'

It was a role that Bill enjoyed unashamedly: 'One of the things that attracted me to the project was the sophisticated way it deals with emotions; it is a grown-up script. I think it is interesting that Dan is portrayed as a likeable and reasonable man without judgment or comment on his homophobia. He is one of those people who have accepted a viewpoint without ever really thinking about it. I think his views would be easily exploded, if the true, loving and important relationship that these two men had was revealed to him.'

His enthusiasm for the project was shared. He won great acclaim for the role, with the *Radio Times* commenting: 'Nighy is particularly good, his mumbled, stumbling delivery hiding the depths of his confusion as he attempts to keep a lid on his mid-life crisis. In *Lawless Heart*, language is also shown to be an inadequate comforter and an imperfect conduit for truth.' The *Guardian* remarked: 'Bill Nighy and Tom Hollander's understated performances – as the deceased's dull brother-in-law and the bereaved boyfriend, respectively – are a joy, bringing quiet dignity to a mature and sharply observant tale.' A BBC Films reviewer stated: 'Yet, *Lawless Heart* instantly grabs your attention through the doleful performance of Bill Nighy, whose mid-life crisis story opens the narrative. "I once faked a broken heart, but I ran out of energy," this downtrodden bar-room philosopher says, before launching into a hesitant attempt at an extra-marital affair.'

Meanwhile, another reviewer from accessatlanta.com wrote: 'The film is beautifully acted. Nighy brings a slightly defeated air, a slightly distracted manner and a touch of the young Peter O'Toole to his role. He makes us believe Dan is someone who could actually say, "I once faked a broken heart, but I ran out of energy."' The *Scotland on Sunday* review was similarly enthusiastic: 'Although it's unfair to single anyone out from such a strong cast, Bill Nighy's flirtatious farmer provides constant pleasure as he negotiates the minefield of his own prejudices, greed and timidity.'

His performance earned him Best Actor at the British Independent Film awards.

In *Lucky Break*, written by Stephen Fry and co-starring Bill's *Still Crazy* chum Timothy Spall, prison inmates stage a musical about Nelson – not for any cultural satisfaction, but as a diversion to their plan of escape. Bill plays 'upper-class twit' Roger 'Rog' Chamberlain, whose facial expressions were described by one critic as 'comic gold.' Another commented: 'Nighy pickpockets every scene as the toff who seems too good for prison.'

His biggest success that year, however, was on stage in Joe Penhall's *Blue/Orange*, directed by Roger Michell (of *Notting Hill* fame), which played to sell-out audiences at the Cottesloe Theatre from 30 April to 23 August. It transferred to the Duchess Theatre in April 2001, with a new cast taking over when the run extended from August 2001 to December of that year.

The play is set in a London mental hospital, where a young patient (Chewitel Ejofor) claims he is the son of an African dictator. Bill plays the senior consultant Robert, who uses the boy's problems to support his own theory of black psychosis. His performance won him great reviews. 'Bill Nighy is outstanding as the power-mad senior shrink, moving from apparent affability to ferocious megalomaniac menace,' wrote the *Daily Telegraph*. 'Bill Nighy's consultant is an overwhelming knockout performance. This is an exposé of the compassionate ego in dramatic vehement engagement. Nighy's emotionally and intellectually charged acting is stamped with naturalness and conviction. Each nuance of the role, from passion to swaggering vanity, is discovered,' sang the *Evening Standard* (which gave *Blue/Orange* its Best New Play and Chewitel Ejofor the Outstanding Newcomer Award). 'Bill Nighy is excellent as the senior consultant whose willowy assurance gives way to bursts of throttled incoherent rage,' wrote the *Guardian*.

In short, he gave a killer performance, most worthy of the Olivier Award nomination for Best Actor that he received (along with Michael Gambon and Simon Russell Beale, with the Award eventually going to relative newcomer Conleth Hill for his performance in *Stones In His Pockets*). *Blue/Orange* won the Olivier

Award for Best Play and the Critics' Circle award for Best Play.

In 2002, Bill got to star alongside his partner Diana Quick for the first time in nearly 20 years, in *AKA* (Diana was also seen in two episodes of TV police drama *Dalziel and Pascoe* that year). Set in England in 1978, *AKA* opens with working-class teenager Dean (Matthew Leitch) thrown out of his home by his abusive father. He then finds work with Lady Gryffoyn (Diana Quick), who introduces him to her society crowd, but then gets rid of the troublesome lad. In an attempt to stay in with the glittering circles, Dean pretends to be Lady Gryffoyn's son Alex and relocates to Paris. There, he makes the acquaintance of Benjamin (Peter Youngblood Hills), a cute, but drug-riddled American, and Benjamin's lover, David (George Asprey), an older playboy who has the hots for Dean. Deceit, class warfare and the complexities of sexual identity unfold. Bill had the humble role of one of Lady Gryffoyn's relatives, Uncle Louis Gryffoyn.

AKA was screened at the 2002 Philadelphia Gay and Lesbian International Film Festival.

That same year, he returned to television in an episode of *The Inspector Lynley Mysteries*, playing the headmaster of a boys' school, but more importantly, he appeared in six episodes of Dick Clement and Ian La Frenais' *Auf Wiedersehen, Pet* with Jimmy Nail and his old friend, Timothy Spall. The show had enjoyed two hugely successful series in the 1980s and in this new series, which transferred to BBC1, Bill plays Jeffrey

Grainger, a disgraced MP who spends time in jail with Oz Osbourne (Jimmy Nail). Grainger's plan was to pull down the Middlesborough Transporter Bridge and sell it. When the original buyer pulls out, an American purchases it instead. The lads, also comprising Kevin Whately, Tim Healy, Christopher Fairbank and Pat Roach (who sadly died shortly afterwards), ended up in a wooden hut just as they had done in the first series except this time in America, not Germany. *Auf Wiedersehen, Pet* enjoyed a run of 12 new episodes and a two-part Christmas special.

Following this came *Ready When You Are, Mr. McGill*, a remake of a comedy first made in 1976, which was directed by Paul Seed. In the new version, Tom Courtenay played McGill, a film extra with just one line, while Bill was the egotistical director.

Bill didn't know it then, but world acclaim was just around the corner. A year later, he would become a household name and finally, deservedly, make his acting mark. But for him, nothing would ever demystify the complexities of acting – or the painful angst each time of going on stage or appearing in front of a camera. Trying to explain it all, he once told a journalist: 'There's an awfully good bit in David Mamet's book *Heresy and Common Sense for the Young Actor*, where he says the quote-character-unquote does not exist because the quote-character-unquote is only a series of black-and-white markings on a page. This prompted Melvyn Bragg to ask him if this meant he was dismissing 70 years of psychological acting and Mamet left a long, beautiful pause before he answered. "Yup," he said. He also addressed the problem of self-consciousness for actors. They could ward it off by hanging garlic around their necks. And that's it. With acting, you have to do everything with the wind-up.'

Chapter Five

'Mack'ing It Big

Playing an ex-addict, washed-up rock star in 2003 was to catapult Bill into a new kind of stardom. He revelled in the role of cynical Billy Mack, an ex-rocker brought back into the public eye with a self-confessed 'festering turd of a record' in *Love Actually*. The Richard Curtis movie had all the feel-good elements (aside from one unfaithful husband, his stalwart wife and a young man desperately in love with his best friend's girl, that is) needed for a Christmas box-office smash.

Despite some of cinema's biggest names – Hugh Grant, Emma Thompson, Alan Rickman, Liam Neeson, Keira Knightley and Colin Firth – wrapped up in the bitter-sweet relationship stories, it was Bill's portrayal of Mack making a bid for the Christmas No. 1 with his contorted version of the sixties' hit, *Love is All Around*, that made the film very much his. As it was, *Christmas Is All Around* did make No. 26 for all of a week in the British charts that year, with some of the proceeds going to Comic Relief. In *Love Actually*, the song reaches No. 1, with Mack's very open disdain and loathing for the tastes of the great British public sending it soaring. According to Bill, his singing 'skills' were based on a combination of Gary Glitter and Elvis Costello.

In fact, he was highly conscious of the veritable pool of stars that he was dipping into in *Love Actually*, causing him to comment about one of his first readings with the cast: 'If a bomb dropped on the warehouse where they all were, it would have wiped out some of the biggest stars in British showbusiness!'

But it was his self-mocking Mack (originally intended to be called Billy Manne and referred to as that in early cast interviews) and the contrast between his objectionable public face and lonely private one that captured the imagination. Billy may have been back on top, but he had no one to share Christmas with, except his long-suffering manager, played by Gregor Fisher.

As one reviewer commented: 'Supposed to be more of a gimmick character, Billy Mack turned out to be the talk of the town. Fans of Emma Thompson, Alan Rickman, Liam Neeson and Colin Firth entered the cinema, Bill Nighy fans were leaving it.'

Indeed, for him, there was some amazing dialogue:

DJ: *Well, thanks for that, Bill.*

Billy Mack: *For what?*
DJ: *Well, for actually giving a real answer to a question. Doesn't often happen here on Radio Watford, I can tell you.*
Billy Mack: *Ask me anything you like, I'll tell you the truth.*
DJ: *Uh... best shag you've ever had?*
Billy Mack: *Britney Spears.*
DJ: *Wow!*
Billy Mack: *No, only kidding... She was rubbish!*
Mikey, DJ interviewer: *How do you think the new record compares to your old classic stuff?*
Billy Mack: *Oh, come on, Mikey, you know as well as I do the record's crap!*
[laughs]
Billy Mack: *...but wouldn't it be great if No. 1 this Christmas wasn't some smug teenager but an old ex-heroin addict searching for a comeback at any price? All those young popsters, come Christmas Day... they'll be stretched out naked with a cute bird balancing on their balls, and I'll be stuck in some dingy flat with me manager, Joe, ugliest man in the world, fucking miserable because our fucking gamble didn't pay off! So, if you believe in Father Christmas, children, like your Uncle Billy does, buy my festering turd of a record! And particularly enjoy the incredible crassness of the moment when we try to squeeze an extra syllable into the fourth line.*
Mikey: *I think you're referring to 'If you really love Christmas...'*

Billy Mack: *'Come on and let it snow...?' Ouch!*
Mikey: *So, uh, here it is one more time, the dark horse for this year's Christmas No. 1, 'Christmas Is All Around'. Thank you, Billy. After this, the news: is the new Prime Minister in trouble already?*

And the critics loved his performance: 'Aside from all the hearts and flowers, though, it's Bill Nighy's uproarious turn as an over-the-hill rocker promoting a novelty record that really delivers the laughs,' said the *Radio Times*. In the *Guardian*, Peter Bradshaw wrote: 'The good news about *Love Actually* is that Nighy is barnstormingly brilliant, hilarious in every scene with a cracker of a laugh in every line. His performance, full of twitches, flinches and naughty-boy grins, is pitch-perfect. And his final mumbling declaration of non-sexual love for his manager, played by Gregor Fisher, interspersed with embarrassed air guitar arm-movements, is the funniest and sweetest thing I've seen on screen all year.' The *Scotsman* stated: 'The connecting thread in the film provides some of the funniest moments, thanks in part to a wonderful comic performance from Bill Nighy as ageing pop idol.' Another review hailed Bill's performance as 'the best, hands down', while yet another described it as 'a comedic delight... It's also a fabulous send-up of any rock star who hasn't realised he's well past his sell-by date. Nighy clearly thoroughly enjoys hamming it up to within an inch of his acting life.'

Love Actually was released on 7 November 2003

and grossed almost £3.5m in its opening weekend. Worldwide, the box offices raked in £123,231,134 during the run, with £29.7m taken in the UK alone, making it the biggest British movie of that year.

Bill won a BAFTA for Best Performance by an Actor in a Supporting Role for his portrayal of Mack, the Peter Sellers Award for Comedy and an ALFS award (London Critics Circle Film Awards). Receiving the ALFS award, he commented: 'With comedy, it's not a dispute – it's either funny or it's not funny and I guess this award means it was funny.'

He also scooped a LAFCA (Los Angeles Film Critics Association) Award and was nominated for a Golden Satellite Award. In 2004, he performed *Christmas is All Around* for two Comic Relief fund-raising events. Then, in May he got together with Radiohead for an event organised by actor Tom Hollander in aid of the children's hospice, Helen House. This took place at the Playhouse in Oxford (the band's home town) and was a star-packed occasion, with comedians Steve Coogan, Rory Bremner and Griff Rhys-Jones and actors Jeremy Irons, Sir Michael Gambon, Hugh Laurie and Francesca Annis among those taking part. Hollander became involved with Helen House when his niece, born with brain damage, was cared for there. Radiohead's performance with Bill was the evening's finale. 'There's a frustrated rock'n' roller inside me,' he wryly remarked.

For the first time ever, he broke his golden rule and watched himself on screen in *Love Actually*. He liked the film, but he wasn't sure about his involvement in it: 'It was good fun, but I thought, "God you're old, you're knackered-looking, you look terrible" – because I do, and I am.'

'I never watch my own films,' he has stated several times. 'I don't know how other actors do it. I know actors are supposed to, but if I can possibly avoid it, I do. I just can't. I don't know why everyone isn't the same. There is nothing in it for me to watch myself. All I see is how far short it falls from what was going on in my head, or what I was attempting, and I don't need that information; I would rather live without that information.

'There was one occasion when I was with my daughter when she was younger and I took her to see a movie and it was too weird for her to see her father hanging out in the lobby. I couldn't rationalise it: "Well, Dad goes away now because he finds the sight of himself physically repulsive." You can't really explain that to a child. "What is wrong, Daddy?" Well, you can hardly respond with, "It makes me nauseous when I lay eyes upon my own image." You can't do that. She held my hand the whole way through it and every time I came on, she just squeezed my hand. That worked.'

But he should not have had such self-doubts and anxieties about *Love Actually*. This was the film that made him. Referring to the famous line he spouts during an Ant and Dec interview for children's TV, he says: 'When I die, they'll put on my gravestone: "Hey kids, don't buy drugs, become a rock star and they give you them for free!"

'The children in the flats near me used to shout that whenever I'd pop to the shops, but it was great: it made me more useful, more castable. You could put me in films in a way that you couldn't before. I'd have been on the list, but way down. Now maybe I'm a bit higher because I'm more familiar to people. I should buy Richard Curtis dinner for the rest of my life – giving me that role with those jokes fundamentally changed the way I work and the pattern of my professional life.'

The mutual respect between Curtis – 'that rare, extraordinary man' – and Bill is evident. According to Curtis: 'One of the great secrets about Bill is that while he dresses so smartly and looks such a gentleman, he's really a sad rock'n'roll fanatic and in some ways that part was his secret self. He's kind of the actor's actor here in England, I think, because he led a really distinguished, slightly edgy theatre career. Then, in *Love Actually*, suddenly he's become a star and the most in-demand actor of all. That's every actor's dream: to have a second, brilliant act. If I were a studio executive, I think the luckiest thing you could do for yourself would be to have Bill get a happy ending in something.'

Another optimistic element of *Love Actually* was that it gave him some feeling of confidence: 'You come to realise there is this huge disparity between what you think about yourself and your work and what other people think about you and your work. At first, you either think they're insane or that it's a conspiracy to make you look stupid. Or maybe, just maybe, they're right and you're sometimes quite good at what you do.'

Love Actually also gave him a profile in America. Until then, he was little known there. 'To them, I'm the newcomer and so when I was in *Variety*, they had to "introduce" me. A friend sent me the cutting and he attached this note that said, "I'm glad to see your career is finally taking off!"'

He himself was a little mystified by the incredible success, but he would be the first to say that any 'feel-good' movie can only ever be good: 'What do you want? Feel-*bad* movies? It's like when people speak about comfort food. I like comfort food, beans and chips, and the type of plain, great food my Irish grandmother used to make. People say, "Oh yes, comfort food", and they say it in a patronising way, like "I used to be like you, but I'm over that now."'

Of course, he could never have envisaged that *Love Actually* would be the making of him. Before its release and subsequent enthusiastic reception, it was just another of the year's projects. He told Australian interviewer Kerry O'Brien: 'It didn't entirely surprise me, it was a year where I did several jobs and I knew if they all went off and were as popular as I imagined they might be, and it would conclude with *Love Actually* at the end of the year, I knew that it could possibly make a change to the way that I go to work.

And in fact, it did. More people probably, definitely, saw me in *Love Actually* than had seen me in everything else I'd ever done in the whole of my career. So it opened up, and that largely means America.

'So what it did was it meant that I became "castable" in American terms, and that was – that's a fundamental change. The biggest, I suppose, the biggest practical difference is that I no longer had to go begging for work; I didn't have to audition for things. Auditioning for actors is humiliating and shaming. And it's one of the worst parts of being an actor, and I did it for 25 years. And you audition 100 times a year, if you're lucky, or whatever it is, and you get six of them. So the rest of the time people tell you to go away, and you know, they can't use you, and it is – it's gruelling, and relentless. And to have that removed, which is what *Love Actually* did for me, is a beautiful thing.'

Later, he admitted that he could only speculate on why it became perhaps the biggest hit of 2003 – and an oft-repeated favourite on television: 'I figure it's because it's a big, big friendly, good-hearted movie with some very nice jokes. And you know, it does make you feel slightly better after seeing it. The character, Billy Mack, does provoke an affection and fondness for those kinds of guys who are still standing and who do kind of speak whatever comes into their mind out of their mouth. Richard Curtis writes some of the best jokes in the world. I know people have *Love Actually* parties and things, and they break out the wine. And because it's a Christmas movie, obviously to some extent it rolls around every year, so it's become like an old friend. And it's one of those movies that people dip into and then they stay there because they don't want to leave.'

One person who doesn't watch the movie at Christmas is Bill himself, though. Apart from his intense dislike of watching himself on screen, he detests that time of year, which he describes as 'scheduled fun.'

The success of *Love Actually* ended a landmark year for him. In May he had appeared alongside Tara Fitzgerald in *I Capture the Castle*, based on Dodie Smith's novel and directed by Tim Fywell. Set in the 1930s, the film follows 17-year-old Cassandra Mortmain (played by newcomer Romola Garai) and the fortunes of her eccentric family, struggling to survive in a decaying English castle. There is a bit of a love rivalry between the two sisters (Rose Mortmain is played by Rose Byrne). Bill is James Mortmain, a chronically depressed and insecure writer, who hasn't written anything in the twelve years since the spectacular success of his first novel. Nor has he fully recovered from the death of his first wife (Tara plays the stepmother), blaming himself after he lunged at her with a cake knife in a sudden rage when he knew she was so ill.

He said of his role: 'It was very tough gig playing a genius surrounded by beautiful women...Very hard being married to Tara Fitzgerald and living in a castle, not easy. I make it look easy, but... I hadn't read the book before but I met lots of women who told me it was in their top five novels of all time. That made me rather nervous, especially because I was playing a man who's supposed to be brooding and charismatic – all the things I know I'm not. That's enough to put the wind up any actor who's got any sense. But I've met several people since who are devotees of the book, who have seen the film and none of them have hit me!'

Released on 7 November, *I Capture the Castle* captured more great reviews for Bill:

'Feverish with hope and desperation, Nighy leaves a lasting impression as the father consumed by a sense of his disappointment,' wrote the *Scotsman*. He also won another LAFCA award for Best Supporting Actor for his role as Mortmain. It was a highly satisfying experience all round, with Bill commenting that the film 'was one of the nicest I've ever done.'

But did he read those rave reviews? The answer is no, he gave all that up a long time ago. 'I never read reviews anymore. I used to say that I didn't read reviews and then sometimes sneak a look. Then I got burned; now I really don't read reviews…'

After this came Stephen Poliakoff's film for the BBC, *The Lost Prince*. It was the tale of Prince John, the son of King George V, who suffered learning difficulties and epilepsy and was hidden away at the royal residence at Sandringham. For Bill, this role had some poignancy. He is official spokesman for the National Society for Epilepsy and has always stressed how important disability and mental health issues are to him.

In *The Lost Prince*, he co-starred with Tom Hollander

and Miranda Richardson (George V and Queen Mary) and played Lord Stamfordham, the King's brilliantly adept private secretary bound by protocol as the country is drawn into World War One. He described his character thus: 'Stamfordham was able to protect George from too much contact with his not altogether supportive government. He could also translate the monarch's wishes into diplomatic terms and convey them to the Prime Minister. He proved a vital conduit between the King and the outside world; everything went through him. He was unquestioningly loyal. You could call Stamfordham the ultimate professional.

'There was a great deal in Poliakoff's screenplay that I didn't know... Lots of things surprised me – like how the First World War actually started. I'm very interested in the accidental nature of history. We imagine that history is the result of careful planning, but often it turns on purely random events. This drama bears that out.

'It wasn't a conventional period piece. It featured the most significant events in our recent history, but that's not the point. Poliakoff has a talent for making a story authentic and universal. This resonates beyond the historical context, so that we, as modern-day viewers, can identify with the characters and understand our history better. There are absolutely no clichés in this work. You'd expect a historical drama to be full of hackneyed ideas, but this is a really fresh view of the past. Poliakoff sees the world in a compassionate and unique way.'

His approach to acting seems somewhat laid-back compared to his fellow performers. There's his lack of 'process' and a non-desire to get into character: 'I don't really know what "character" means – it's not an altered state for me, it's not a trance. I don't really know what people mean when they say "in character". I'm at work, I don't know pretending. It's not psychiatric, not for me. Maybe it is for some people, I'm sure it might be for some people. Most people I know, yes. I've never worked with an actor who became someone else.

'I don't know what the expression means, "becoming someone else". I mean, it's not psychologically impossible, I don't think. Maybe there are people who do it, I don't know. Every actor I've ever worked with is of course the same person once the camera stops rolling as they are the time while the camera is rolling. They haven't changed in any way, it's only tricks and a bit of feeling, but mostly just tricks. I don't know what "in character" means 'cause I've never been in character – I've been at work acting. You don't change in any way.'

Acting, whatever, the basis certainly works for the excellent reviews continued with *The Lost Prince*: 'Personally, I can't get enough of Nighy. Close your eyes and just breathe in that voice – it's the aural equivalent of eating dark chocolate truffles dipped in whipped cream,' rhapsodised the *Guardian*.

He won a Golden Satellite Award for his role as Baron Stamfordham. The film achieved high viewing figures and won further praise. It was released on VHS and DVD, then repeated on BBC1 in January 2004. A further repeat showing followed on BBC2 in January 2006. Both Miranda Richardson and Gina McKee received Best Actress nominations at the British Academy Television Awards in April 2004. The mini-series was also nominated for BAFTA TV awards for editing (Clare Douglas), music (Adrian Johnston) and photography (Barry Ackroyd).

When the production was transmitted in the US in October 2004, it won the Emmy Award for Outstanding Mini Series in 2005. Miranda Richardson was nominated for a Golden Globe. It was interesting to note that in early publicity for *The Lost Prince*, pre-*Love Actually*, Bill did not even get a cast mention. Sadly, neither did his 18-year-old daughter Mary, who played the 'young Mary' in her very first TV appearance. It was inevitable that she would join her parents in an acting career, something she had always wanted. Besides, she was to say, in true self-effacing Nighy style: 'I could tell from my school records that I was never going to be a scientist!'

Bill followed *The Lost Prince* up with a six-part TV dramatisation of Paul Abbott's *State of Play*, a thriller set in London, in which a politician's life becomes ever more complex when his research assistant is found dead on the Underground. It's not long before rumours of an affair hit the headlines and, in a seemingly unrelated incident, a teenage drug dealer is shot dead.

Starring alongside David Morrissey as the politician

Stephen Collins and John Simm as investigative journalist Cal McCaffrey, Bill dazzled as the screamingly funny and sarcastic Cameron Foster. Editor of the *Herald* newspaper investigating the case, he is hell-bent on giving no co-operation to the police whatsoever and very little assistance to his arrogant journalist son, played by James McAvoy. There was also the endless supply of wine at editorial meetings.

And he loved the role, describing his character as 'a decent man in a hard game', who 'absolutely believes in the benign power of newspapers. He seems to have survived the experience of having worked in Fleet Street in an admirable way. He's honest and he does think that if you bring information into the world, it is with a view to making things better.'

In fact, he was so enthralled that he read the entire six hours' worth of script in one sitting: 'I got up to put the kettle on once, you know, it was gripping and I knew I had a good role...'

State of Play was directed by David Yates (the man behind the *Harry Potter* movies) and described by Bill (with whom he worked on *The Girl in the Café*) as 'one of the most gifted directors I've ever worked with.'

Above all, the role gave him another chance to act out the part of newspaperman, even though he himself had never actually made one in real life. He was delighted to have been 'promoted', albeit only on-screen: 'I played seven journalists when I was a young man – it became a running joke when I was in my thirties – but never an editor. I'm going up in the world!' he laughed.

Laughing too was scriptwriter Paul Abbott, who described Bill as 'fantastic', adding: 'He's somebody who can step into complex occupational roles, whether it be a rock musician or newspaper editor, and play the parts convincingly.'

Certainly, he had a ball as Cameron Foster, blessed with such lines as: 'Hands up anyone who's never screwed a source', 'Why don't you go and type something lovely?' as he hustles a reporter out of his office and 'It's not a question of whether I'm right or wrong. I'm the boss – just do it!'

As the *Guardian*'s TV critic, Kathryn Flett, noted: 'Nighy manages to do that brilliant thing of not appearing to act. You can imagine walking into a newspaper office and seeing him sitting there, doing that job. What's more, you can't imagine anyone else playing the part.'

One strange phenomenon was that he received letters from people who had worked on *The Times* asking if they could come and work with him! As he recalls, 'It was very popular with journalists because they were seen in a positive way. Usually, like actors, they are brought in to represent something else. In this, they were responsible and principled. And I was very popular with journalists because at one point I got to pick up the phone and say, "Hold the front page!" which everyone got very excited about.'

His empathy with the role helped him scoop a BAFTA award in May 2004. Strangely, it was nearly five years before *State of Play* was released on DVD in the US, the country that now idolised him, but the February 2008 release was much appreciated by fans and critics alike, with the *Chicago Tribune* saying, 'The mini series is worth watching just to see Nighy steal every scene he's in...'

In the eyes of both big- and small-screen critics, he could do no wrong. The year 2003 was certainly proving to be a major one. The *Guardian* summed up his success in *State of Play* (hailing Bill as having 'the sexiest voice on TV') and other ventures that year: 'And then suddenly we were in the mood for a proper drama like the fabulous *State of Play*, the first of Bill "God" Nighy's three hits for 2003, alongside *Love Actually* and (though he may not consider it his greatest dramatic stretch) a very funny turn on *Grumpy Old Men*.'

The latter was a reference to the BBC 'Talking Heads' series in which the likes of Bill, Bob Geldof, Richard Madeley, Arthur Smith, Rory McGrath, John Peel, Geoffrey Palmer, Rick Stein, Tony Hawks and Ken Stott took up the challenge of moaning with relish about everything that's wrong in this modern world. The series was the brainchild of executive producer Stuart Prebble, who one day realised if he got angry about most elements of 21st-century living, there must be others who did, too.

At first the BBC was reluctant to call the series *Grumpy Old Men* because executives believed no one in their right mind would want to be labelled as such. Prebble recalls: 'I responded that if people were not happy to identify themselves under this heading, then they were definitely not what we were looking for. Grumpy Old Men know exactly who they are and are not at all reluctant to admit that they are one.'

He did, however, receive vehement refusals from 'all sorts of people you might expect to jump at the sobriquet.' Arthur Smith was first on board, closely followed by journalist Will Self and Rick Wakeman. Bob Geldof was initially too grumpy to appear, but then reluctantly agreed as a personal favour and enjoyed himself so much that he recruited TV boss Michael Grade to take part. Said Prebble: 'It turned out later that Michael was doing it in a craven attempt to approve his chances of being appointed chairman of the BBC, but we didn't know it at the time. Much as Bill Nighy used it as a springboard to get the part in *Love Actually*. We made these people what they are today, but do they thank us? Well, that's another story… Rory McGrath, John O'Farrell, Rick Stein, John Peel, Bill Nighy, they all recognised the phenomenon straightaway.'

Bill appeared in four episodes titled: 'Is This the World We Created?', 'Stuff', 'A Day in the Life' and 'So Who's To Blame?' The series gave men of a certain age the chance to damn all that's modern and wrong with society today. Everything from the IKEA stores to music tinkling from personal headphones was blasted. Bill, of course, had a ball in his usual laconic way, combining self-effacement with things he just did not understand. Prebble recalls with glee how he appeared in front of the cameras: '...then a little-known ballet dancer and announced that he had no plans for a penile extension.'

One of Bill's musings was about breakfast TV: 'Well, I suppose the media is such a major industry now and it needs feeding, so rather than wait for celebrity to happen, they sort of invent it in order to report on it. Do you know what I mean? You don't necessarily have to wait any more. You just make it up as you go along.'

Celebrity chef Rick Stein described how he found it amusing how men apparently constantly worry about having the 'largest willy' but are preoccupied with having the smallest phone at the same time. Bill agreed, saying that as long has he had the smallest possible phone, he didn't care what make it was. However, in real life he is greatly adored by the young and not completely against all things technical. He even has an iPod, though he has to persuade friends to load it up with music!

He rarely rants – he is simply not the type, except during a rare explosion of morning temper if he can't plug the kettle in first time, can't get one of his jackets off a hanger or if a cupboard door won't open properly. Any of those can make him 'bloody rattled' and cause him to break clothes hangers for their sheer lack of co-operation. Mostly, he just delivers his pronouncements in a way that makes you think he has a point. He did this when a journalist asked what annoys him about the world. Bill answered: 'I'm going to irritate the rest of Britain and say the English

Channel. I think we should just hunker down with the rest of Europe and get on with things. I don't think it's improved our manners, being that far out to sea. And I might bring Ireland a bit closer and have bridges... so we could walk there. I thought we could bring the temperature down in the Middle East just a touch; maybe make it a little cooler round there, see if that works... and maybe a little more rainfall in California. And replace the paintings and churches in Florence that were lost through the flood and to bring back the things from the wars – to restore all those beautiful buildings and paintings to their former glory.'

Cyclists, too, annoy the hell out of him: 'As a pedestrian it drives me nuts – they whizz past you. If you scratched your head, they'd either break your arm or you'd knock them out. They're not proper cyclists, you know. They are frightened of traffic.'

In an interview with Susan Daly for the *Irish Independent*, he also admitted that social networking site Facebook was his idea of a nightmare: 'The idea that you enumerate your friends makes me want to kill myself right there.' The existence of Twitter appalls him too. No matter that celebrities such as Stephen Fry and Jonathan Ross keep the public informed of their every (and often trivial) movement on the site: 'They don't tell people that they are going to do their laundry? Why would they do that?' Aside from being strongly opposed to revealing his private life to thousands of strangers, Bill just doesn't relish being embarrassed. Ask him about his musical hates and he will answer, 'Techno death thrash metal, tramp jazz and anything where the drummer has got brushes.' Among his favourites, however, are Marvin Gaye (particularly the album *Praise*), Aretha Franklin's 'A Rose is Still a Rose', Johnny 'Guitar' Watson's 'Hook Me Up' and Prince's 'Damn U'. 'It's the sweetest slice of romantic soul imaginable,' he said of his choice.

He loathes holidays too: 'I hate my inability to enjoy myself. I just hate the feeling that I'm supposed to be having a really good time. And I hate the sun, seafood, exhibitions and sights. I don't want to see the sights!'

And you won't find him on a beach either. He hates them too! This could have something to do with a traumatising moment when he was a young man on a romantic holiday. 'I took to the beach in a singlet. I turned pink in the sun and when I took the singlet off, its shadow remained. I felt so ashamed. I haven't been to the beach in a long time; I have no need to go to the beach. I've been working, that's my excuse. I was working and I couldn't make it to the beach,' he told *Sunday Times* journalist Ariel Leve, confessing in mock Cockney that he wasn't the world's greatest swimmer, anyway. 'We didn't 'ave a lot of swimmin' round our way. I don't remember anyone goin' swimmin'. I did think about learning to swim – but then I put the kettle on and had a double espresso.' When Leve asked what would happen then he was drowning and Bill was the only one around, Bill replied 'You'd die...Well, no – I'd have a go.'

He is proud of his country, but will say: 'Like most

people, I do have a button marked "Patriotism". Let's just say that I'm choosy who I'm allowing to press it – certainly not politicians and certainly not the Queen.' But he is genuinely proud of Britain's weather – he likes the seasonal changes, he loves storms. For him, a perfect nocturnal pastime is to sit in front of a window on a wet and windy night, the kind where tree branches strike the glass: 'It gets me going.'

Britain has weather, other countries don't, he declares. That's one reason why he would never live in the 'La La Land' that is Los Angeles, for instance. 'Imagine me in Los Angeles. You open the curtains and you know nothing's going to happen. It's going to be precisely how it was yesterday and the day before that. So, after a while it gets to be deeply unsettling – they don't get no weather. I dig the weather more than anything else. The only weather I don't like is, well, I'm not mad about the heat. I don't understand the impulse to rush out. I mean, I am never going to take my shirt off. That's never going to happen.'

But when it comes to putting the world to rights, he has a very personal dream. To put Crystal Palace 'in the semi-finals of the European Cup.' For many years, he has been an ardent fan and since 2004 has been patron of the CPFRIS (Crystal Palace FC Fast Results & Information Service) Disabled Children's Club.

Formed in 1998, the Club became a charity in 2001. Now it funds and organises Christmas parties for around 200 disabled children. There was also enough money donated to hire an executive box at Crystal

Palace's Selhurst Park ground, enabling disabled kids and their carers from schools and societies in south London to see matches in a secure environment. Everyone involved in the charity is a volunteer and as patron, Bill combines his two greatest passions: Crystal Palace and children. 'Kids are the meaning of life,' he says. 'That, and Crystal Palace Football Club.'

Whether or not his team are playing, Bill whiles away those long periods on set in between filming by watching a good game. He finds the sight of skilful play almost an art form: 'I don't really mind who's playing. What you do is, you sit and wait for passages of great beauty. You wait for someone – the rare individual – who will do something in a billionth of a moment. It's over before anyone can do the maths. You have to see it in slow motion to get the physics. There are players able to achieve something that very few people can. It involves great elegance and intelligence and grace – that's when I get seriously interested. Zola, Beckham, Berbatov... these are people who can achieve incredible things, but make it beautiful as they do it.'

In fact, most of his ambitions revolve around football. He told travel writer Caroline Shearing of the *Telegraph*: 'I want to go on a train to Paris to watch a Paris Saint Germain football match and then stay overnight at the Ritz. The next day, I'd take a sleeper train to Madrid, travelling first-class, to see Real Madrid play. I'd visit Milan to see AC Milan, Rome to watch AS Roma, Munich for Bayern Munich,

Barcelona for FC Barcelona, Turin to see Juventus FC – and I'd probably end up watching Galatasaray in Istanbul. I'd take in all the great European clubs, while living and sleeping on a train, and I'd get a hat or a shirt from each one.'

He would still prefer to watch a Champions League game, though, with just its opening music bringing him 'peace' rather than some of the biggest foreign clubs: 'International football involves lots of other people worrying about things that don't concern me, like where they come from.'

2003 was not just about *Love Actually*, but Hollywood actually too. Before *Love Actually*'s Christmas release, Bill made his blockbuster debut that September in *Underworld*, playing Viktor, a vampire 'elder' who has been asleep for centuries and then appears in menacing human form. His co-star was Kate Beckinsale, playing a beautiful vampire warrior (Selene), entrenched in the war between the vampire and werewolf races. Although in league with the vampires, she falls in love with Michael Corvin (Scott Speedman).

Later, there would be two other *Underworld* films, which thrilled a vampire-lover Bill: 'They wear groovy clothes, they stay up late – you know what I mean? They never go to bed. They sleep in the daytimes, they sometimes sleep upside down, they drink blood, which is kind of cool – usually, extraordinarily, from the necks of beautiful women which I kind of, I don't know, find strangely moving.'

He told journalist Rebecca Murray: '...And it's so kind of sexy. There's obviously something about the biting of a woman's neck and drinking her blood. I don't know where anyone else stands, but I hope it's not just me, but it is obviously erotic. But there's something about that fact that it's almost, could almost be true. You know what I mean? They're nearly plausible, the idea that there's a race of people that exists and nourish themselves simply on other peoples' blood of young people or whatever.'

Underworld was directed by Len Wiseman and co-written with Kevin Grevioux. According to Wiseman, Bill was, 'amazed to get the gig.' His audition day had not started well. It was a steamy summer London morning and Bill was slogging about the city on the London Underground when someone threw themselves under the Tube train he was travelling on. 'I had to get off the Tube and everyone was quiet and awful,' he recalls. 'And then I remember having to walk for miles and miles to get to the place where I was meeting Len for the first time.'

With typical cynicism, he shrugged off his audition as doing 'my version of a vampire' before walking away and thinking, 'That will be the end of that. There was just this very nice man, Len, with a camcorder saying, "Would you like to do the scene now?" and he gave me the gig, more or less on the spot. That was nice because you get used to just walking away and thinking they won't happen.

'But I did admire the script, I was very keen. I

thought the script was as hip and as cool a script, a vampire/werewolf script, as you'll ever find anywhere in the world. And they're believers, you know – they're real enthusiasts. They didn't just make a vampire movie because they were trying to get into the movies or something and it was their first movie, they chose very carefully. It was the movie that they wanted to make and they wanted it to be their first movie. And it went straight in at No. 1 in America and made a whole bunch of money, and they're really, really, really, really nice guys, so I was thrilled.'

The role called for him to spend 6 hours each day patiently being made up for the character that was meant to be 1,000 years old. He recalls: 'Had I known what the thousand-year-old bit meant, if I truly knew what being asleep for 1,000 years meant, I would never have turned up! They put me in a prosthetic trunk with these very nice guys who, for 6 hours, apply – with industrial adhesive – chunks of latex to your body so that you can barely move. They then put contact lenses in and fangs, and then nobody will have lunch with you anymore. It's horrible, there's nothing good about it!

'First of all, they fly you to Los Angeles and pour a bucket of alginate over your head, and just before they pour the bucket, the young man says, "Um... do you get... like... claustrophobic or anything?" and it is a little late for that, actually. They put things up your nose so you can breathe and then they wait for it to harden. You can feel it hardening around your shoulders and head, and they take that off and then they put it all over your torso and you stand up. And they all stop laughing at your jokes because you have to stand up for some time while it hardens around your rib cage, and it all gets a bit spooky and a bit quiet, and you're wondering why it has all gone a bit quiet. And then afterwards they crack you out of it and tell you that half the people faint apparently because it gets so tight around their ribs that they can't breathe properly. They have to catch you when that happens, which is why it all goes a bit quiet. By the time you leave the building they have a full-length model of you and they can do anything to it. They can cut your head off, they can cut your legs off, anything they want.'

But he took it all in his stride, although it is not something, he says, that he would like to repeat too often. It was only his music that kept him sane. Dylan and the Rolling Stones are the two best friends he always relies on. They go everywhere with him, especially when filming: 'I always christen a trailer with the Stones. It's always *Goats Head Soup*, and it's always the second track, "100 Years Ago". Then it goes onto Dylan. It kind of controls the environment. Music's always been ludicrously important to me.'

During the gruelling makeover sessions for *Underworld*, he listened to 'the complete works of the Rolling Stones while they put it on. They said, "Do you have any tunes you like?" I'd just bought the complete works of the Rolling Stones for the third time in my life and I said, "Yeah, I like the Rolling Stones." So they played every tune the Rolling Stones ever did while you stand there and then when they take it off; it brings lumps of flesh with it! So, when they rip it off, they chip it off with stiff brushes and 99 per cent alcohol, like you were wallpapering an old house. This is not helping me to act, there's no part of it that prepared me to play the role or anything like that. It's just awful! You just count the money.'

While enjoying great public success, he quietly achieved a private one that year too. He stopped smoking. The exact day is etched in his memory – 13 September 2003. He says: 'I didn't know if I'd be able to stop smoking, but by some miracle I did. I still haven't got over it. Every day I think, "I don't smoke!"' It was a momentous decision for a man who had smoked for 30 years. 'I would rather have smoked than breathed! You couldn't smoke more than I smoked.'

But the habit was taking its toll on his health – Bill is no good at having vices, he enjoys them with too much passion, as witnessed earlier. Somewhere, somehow, just as it did with his drinking, a small quiet voice comes into his head and he sees sense. It was a health scare while filming *Underworld* that was the catalyst. During a fight scene, he experienced some pain. It was difficult to pinpoint whether this was as a result of moving his shoulder too quickly or something more sinister, but he suffered chest pains, too: 'It goes a bit quiet at my age when you say you have chest pains. I had scary chest X-rays and you go into the room for your results and everything slows down. You think, "It's a little early for all this." And I got scared.'

Of his nicotine addiction, he says it was one of the 'great regrets of my life... If I could say one thing to anybody starting out in life, I would say: "Whatever you do, don't smoke." I have had to recover from that and I have been lucky that I have been able to stop. It's not like having a drink in a normal way – you are in chemical thrall on a metabolic level. Alcohol is arguably the heavyweight champion drug of the world, but nicotine is right up there and it's great to be liberated from nicotine because it's a real bugger – it robs you of so much out of the day.'

He did, however, then develop a sweet tooth, admitting to 'bingeing' his way off cigarettes on fruit gums, Lion bars and Magnum ice creams until completely eliminating refined sugar from his diet in 2009. But then Bill does find it hard not to become addicted to certain things – at one time he drank 18 cans of Diet Coca Cola a day. 'People would just hand it to me when I walked on set, it was embarrassing.'

His next TV project was in the BBC's contemporary take on Chaucer's *Canterbury Tales*, playing the lecherous husband James Dunbar, who provokes the Wife of Bath, 53-year-old Beth Craddock (Julie Walters) into an affair with a young man (Paul Nicholls).

There followed a fascinating television piece when Bill linked up once again in *The Young Visiters* with executive producer Jim Broadbent to play the Earl of Clincham – 'We're going to have a party, a jolly good party. Splendid!'

The story was written in 1891 by 9-year-old Daisy

Ashford. Complete with spelling mistakes and each chapter written as a single paragraph, it was penned in a red exercise book and pulled out of a drawer by Daisy in 1917. The book was eventually published with a foreword by Peter Pan creator J.M. Barrie and became a huge success, reprinting 18 times in its first year alone.

A stage version was first performed in London in 1920, transferring to New York shortly afterwards. The New York production, at the Thirty-Ninth Street Theatre, received good reviews. One reviewer remarked: '*The Young Visiters* has been turned into a play by the simple use of a pair of shears and a pot of paste. Probably no novel was ever so reverently dramatized since the world began.'

The 2003 TV comedy project was a personally satisfying role for Bill. It starred Jim Broadbent as Alfred Salteena, a middle-aged and prosperous ironmonger in Victorian England, in desperate need of female company. He meets and falls in love with Ethel Monticue (Lyndsey Marshal). Alfred then he realises that he needs to go away to swot up on his social techniques, if he is to keep Ethel. He makes the fatal mistake of leaving her in the safe hands of Lord Bernard Clark (Hugh Laurie) while he goes off to a training school for gentlemen, run by a drunken, impecunious aristocrat called the Earl of Clincham, played by... Yes, you've guessed it!

Bill commented: 'I very much enjoyed playing the Earl of Clincham in *The Young Visiters*. I wish that film was more seen. Jim Broadbent is an old friend whom I'm very, very fond of and it was lovely to work with him again. He and I started out together. We've known each other all our lives. Acting with him was extremely satisfying and very, very funny. We were playing kind of comedy tennis.

'I wouldn't mind being the Earl of Clincham. I think he had a pretty good life, sort of nuts and deluded in a perfectly cheerful way. And he lived at Court. I mostly liked that I got to have a fringe – that means the hair that falls down over your eyes. I always wanted a fringe, but I never had the right hair. I got to have a hairpiece, what they call "curtains". You know, when boys have a fringe in front of their eyes with just a little gap like a curtain. It was a fashion for a while. So I got some sort of ancient curtains and got to shake my fringe. I've always wanted to shake my fringe. We just had good fun. I wouldn't mind people running down the street shouting, "Clincham, Clincham!"'

Shown on British television as part of the Christmas viewing fare, on 26 December 2003, *The Young Visiters* won a BAFTA for Best Original Music and aired on American TV screens the following year. *Variety* magazine commented on Bill's Earl of Clincham character as being, 'an amusingly haughty Bill Nighy.'

It was the end of an astonishing year. Bill Nighy, former pupil of the Guildford School of Drama and Dance, was now in demand. For him, it really was '*Love Actually*', as far as his fans were concerned. He told journalist Robert Butler: 'I owe Richard Curtis endless dinners. Richard changed the way I work. *Love Actually* gave me a profile in America, and it meant that I no longer had to sing for my supper. After that movie I was invited to go to work, that's a big change in an actor's life; it is also a bit disorienting. I remember the first few times I went to auditions after *Love Actually* and things were not going right, and it took a while to realise that they were trying to sell me on the job rather than the other way around.'

Insecurity about his own abilities was still there, though: 'I don't know how other people find it, but I know there are some very distinguished actors who have great difficulty persuading themselves on a daily basis that they can actually do their job. Like me, they don't really learn, the history doesn't help – I have to go through precedents. Before I start a job, there's a patch of sky outside my back door and I go and refer to this patch of sky. I sometimes run through the jobs I have done previously, the precedent for me being OK at work, the times when they have asked you back, incontrovertible evidence that you are apparently capable of doing your job. I have to convince myself every time. I am getting better, I am working on it.'

Chapter Six

An Actor's Life

While Bill was enjoying great success, so too was his partner, Diana Quick. It had been a good couple of years for her, too. In 2002, she had gone on the road with the English Touring Theatre's production of Ibsen's *Ghosts*, for which she won both the Barclays/TMA and *Manchester Evening News* Awards for Best Actress. In the spring of 2003, she was back on stage with theatre group Shared Experience in *After Mrs Rochester*, a play based on the life of writer Jean Rhys. She also managed to squeeze in three films; *AKA* (in which she starred with Bill), *Revenger's Tragedy* (with Eddie Izzard and Derek Jacobi) and a Dutch film, *The Discovery of Heaven*, with Greg Wise and Stephen Fry.

By now, the two were reaping the rewards of their respective acting talents. There had never been any competitiveness between them, even when their careers have been out of sync. In the early days of their meeting, it was Diana who made the money. In fact, at one time, Bill – 'the worst driver in the world' – became a mini cab driver to earn some cash: 'When we were first together Diana made all the money and I made absolutely nothing. Both of us have only been grateful for wherever the money was coming from, especially in the early days when we were starting a family. I was just happy that somebody was making money, otherwise we'd have been in serious trouble. She's been my staunchest supporter and encourager.'

Increasing life on the road – and therefore apart – would, however, cost them dear. And then, in between acting work, Bill was fitting in other appearances. There was Channel 4's *The Paul O'Grady Show* and then he took time out to co-host (with Fiona Shaw) the 25th birthday party of the Gate Theatre, one of London's leading fringe venues. The gala event was held at the Twentieth Century Theatre in Notting Hill on 18 March 2004.

In April 2004, he took on a role in *The Moment Theatres Dumped the Musical*, a show put on by a cast with learning disabilities from The Moment By Moment Theatre Company, run and funded by the Yarrow charity. The romantic comedy centred on the trials of Silas, a young farmer who loses his heart to a fickle milkmaid. After her affections are stolen by villain Faisal, the heartbroken Silas tries to forget his loss through drink and general debauchery. Bill plays 'the compromised President of the United States whom Silas meets on his travels.'

Television investigator Donal MacIntyre was a spoof undercover reporter called Doughnut MacIntosh. MacIntyre actually appeared on stage at London's Arts Education School, but because of his work schedule Bill recorded his own contribution, which was projected on a screen during the performance.

The acting company was set up in 2001 by Yarrow to help build the confidence, speech, coordination and social skills of those with learning disabilities, as well as to provide literacy and employment training. Commenting on his involvement with the project, Bill said: 'The last show put on by Yarrow's service users was brilliant and so I was delighted when they asked me to take part in their newest production. Not only are the members of the cast very good actors but I think the Moment by Moment group can also help to educate us all: the public have a lot of misconceptions about people with learning disabilities, which seeing *Dumped* will blow away. It will make you realise that, just because someone has a disability, this doesn't prevent them from being as talented as the next person.'

The charity work that Bill undertakes is incredible for two reasons: first, that he finds time to fit it all in and second, that most of it – which he is more than happy to accept – goes unrecognised. He is highly supportive of causes involving disabled people and children. At the end of 2004, together with actress Imelda Staunton, he launched an appeal for the final £1.6m towards the £12.6m cost of a permanent base for the Unicorn Theatre, Britain's first purpose-built, professional theatre for children. For over 50 years, the theatre has produced plays for young people and its proposed dedicated site, behind the London mayoral headquarters on the South Bank, would include educational facilities.

April also saw a return to period drama in Anthony Trollope's *He Knew He Was Right*, a four-part mini-series adapted by Andrew Davies, a writer famed for sexing up the classics. Bill revelled in his role as the rakish Colonel Osborne, a man who claims to know his way around women. His appeal is unnerving to one young husband, Louis Trevelyan (Oliver Dimsdale), who is convinced his pretty wife Emily (Laura Fraser) has fallen under the Colonel's spell.

'I was in my element,' recalled Bill. 'It had everything – an excellent script from a well-written novel, which observes the dark, the comic and the ridiculous characters around at the time, but it travels through the centuries very well. The egos and emotions can apply to us today, so it all seems fresh.' He was also delighted to see young talent, such as Christina Cole and Stephen Campbell Moore in the production, alongside the likes of reliable veterans Geoffrey Palmer, Geraldine James, John Alderton, Joanna David and James Bolam. Bill noted: 'They all seem so much better than I was at their age. I felt throughout my 20s that I would be found out at any moment, told to stop wasting my time and go out and get a real job.'

He was, however, invited to join the Academy of

Motion Picture Arts and Sciences (AMPAS) so he must have been doing something right!

In May, Bill was announced as the voice behind a £3m advertising campaign for Zanussi Electrolux washing machines. That same month, on 2 May, he took part in a special question-and-answer session at the Haymarket to highlight the Royal Academy of Dramatic Art, which was celebrating its 100th anniversary. For the gathering of young would-be actors, it was a magical experience, with Bill being highly entertaining, self-effacing, cynical and totally honest about his profession. And he raised lots of laughter. Asked about his many thoughts of giving it all up, he replied: 'That is because I have this dangerous mixture of intense vanity and self-loathing, which is not a great way of starting the day. Don't worry, you don't have to be like me, thank God!'

He was also asked about voice projection and this was his detailed answer: 'When you work in the National Theatre, there are three theatres. One is very big, one is quite big and the other one is not big at all. If you start in the Cottesloe – which is the small one – and then you are about to do a play in the Lyttleton – which is the middle one – people always come up, older actors, and say, "Oh, the Lyttleton. You're in trouble now, son." I'd say, "Why am I in trouble?" and they'd say, "Because it's big." They always freak you out.

'But what you actually do is you go in the Cottesloe and you speak so that person up there can hear you.

Then you go on to the Lyttleton and you speak so that person up there can hear you – you just raise your voice slightly. And when you go on at the Olivier, there is a technicality that the audience is over there, and over there, so whatever the line, you start it there and then you spray it across the thing, it's not rocket science. But you do meet people who say, "Oh… the Olivier…" It's like when you go on radio and people say, "How's your microphone technique?" and you go, "What?" That was a double-take by the way – I just did a double-take. This is very important information, I never got taught any of this. I got taught stuff which I now discover is physically and psychologically impossible in the first place and is of no use to either me or the audience.

'I wanted to know stuff like how to do a double-take. So when they put the camera there, you talk as required and you act as required. You are too young to worry about nasal hair. But it will come, I can tell you. You go into makeup and they have this strange thing. Yep, they stick it up your nose! No, you just find that instinctively it is not such a problem. You do kind of instinctively know, like when you were a kid and you were pretending and playing with your friends or your imaginary friends – I had some, I will be the first to say it. And when you are whispering, and when you're being quiet and when the focus is close, then you act accordingly. It sounds very clever now, but the first time I was on telly a very marvellous man called T.P. McKenna, a very distinguished Irish actor, literally used to say, "Favour the camera" and pointed me round to the camera because I would be here and the camera would be there… because I was trying to be like real and I was so freaked out by my personal anxiety that I would get everything right, except where the camera was!

'But everyone has watched the movies. Everybody has seen them and the director will help you. This doesn't sound very expert or anything, but you just kind of know that there are certain things required of you in a big space and not in a little one. If it is a close focus, you will act accordingly. I am always amazed, for instance, when I have done a couple or three plays when you have subsequently had to do them on radio. They have been recorded as productions and you think you are being on stage. You think you are being "natural" and pretty authentic and real. And then they put you in front of a microphone and you discover that everything you have done vocally on stage is of no use to you anymore, ever. I don't really understand it, but it is just the delivery, the intonation, the spirit of the way you have done the line, which will not work anywhere else. And obviously, on camera you are on microphone and the volume of your voice will be monitored by someone else so you don't have to in any way raise your voice or modulate your voice in any way that you wouldn't in real life.

'But you discover there are certain things – it's like when you rehearse in your hotel room. Everyone comes to work having been in horrible hotels in a lousy room and you get the script, which is almost always not very good – this is television – and then you have to go in and deliver one. If I watch popular television and see someone in a popular piece of television really turn one in, I nearly cry because I know they have been in the worst hotel in Nottingham. They gave them the train fare, they gave them food which is not any good and no one talks to them because they've got no social skills in the hotel. And then they turn up and the director just goes, "Oh, hi. Oh God, yeah! Oh, hi. Can you just hang on there for a minute?" And then at some point later in the day they are going to go, "Action!" And you have to deliver one and I am always terribly moved when people do. Often they don't. They do this other thing, which is called being on TV, which is another thing, which is sort of making a personal appearance. It's the opposite thing to acting – a lot of it goes on.

'And I have this theory that because the schedules are so tight and because the budget is so small and therefore everyone is always under terrible pressure, you turn on the television and you have what are perfectly normal exchanges between people, but all of them seem to be cross. Everyone is just slightly pissed off. You'll have someone come in and ask if you would like a cup of coffee and you go, "WHAT? Yeah, I'll have some coffee." Because it's butch, that's what it is. You're under such stress, but you don't know what to do. It gives you a sort of bogus authority. "Oh dear, he's upset. Doesn't he look marvellous when he's angry?"

'I have a friend of mine called Carl Johnson, who is a wonderful actor and a marvellous man, and he is one of the few people I can stand talking about acting to. I can't stand most people talking about acting because I get embarrassed, but he can talk about it and he and I are sort of undercover agents for cheerful acting. It's like when you are young and you've got a fringe, you can hang out... and you can do all that shit. Sean Penn, an actor I admire, when asked about the Brat Pack said, "That isn't acting – that's what you do to get laid!" And he's absolutely right. A lot of that goes on. It's always the guys that do it, mostly. The girls are much braver and much better. But the guys are always pissed off and they do nothing because that's what their favourite actor does. But yes, I am a very small society of undercover actors who attempt to do things cheerfully because it's radical. The conventional thing is to look fucked up whereas we like to be radical and cheerful.

'I don't suppose for a moment that answers your question... but I think you'll find that you talk down to the camera and talk up to the stage and that's it. There isn't any magic thing. And hopefully the director will know what he's doing and will say "Up a bit". They've done that to me and that director makes million-dollar movies. That's what it comes down to – there is no secret thing here. It's what you did as a kid, it's what you did in the bushes. It is not rocket science, but it is really hard sometimes. Certain bits are easier than others. People have their favourite bits because they are the bits that come easiest to them. And when you are young, and the easiest thing – if you were like me, self-conscious and nervous – that comes to you is doing absolutely nothing and attempting to make it look meaningful, which is really boring…'

There was not a day when he didn't consider giving it all up and changing jobs, he told his audience: 'Seriously, every day I have thought about doing something else for a living, particularly early on. Not lately, not for the last 10 years. But I have been doing it for about 30, so there were about 20 years of waking up most mornings and thinking, "You've got to get something to do, this is killing you." I find it incredibly difficult and I am not alone, it is not uncommon. What keeps you at it is that I've got no prospects and I don't do nothing – I can't what, drive a mini cab. That was the early days. There is that moment when your wife turns to you and says, "Well, do something else then." And you go, "Like what?" I famously can't drive – I'm useless in a car.

'But when I think back, I don't know what kept me at it except I hated the idea of saying I had failed. Going back home and saying it didn't come off, I couldn't do that conversation – every now and again, something would give in me and I would arrange to be unguarded long enough for some light to get in so that I could get a touch of humility. That is what you require because humility is a kind of courage and what you require is a funny sort of courage and it has to cease to be all about you. What I tell myself now when

I am doing a play is that there are these people and I'm just one. There's that guy who is the director and he's insane and there's the person who's building this world and that person who's making the music. There are about 28 of us, my name is Bill and I'm one of them. Otherwise it starts to be about me and we are in serious trouble, and that helps diffuse my self-obsession, which is partly a self-consciousness. Everything becomes so important and you become a centre of the universe and you think the audience's focus is entirely on you.

'I did this when I had one line. I was the guy who came on and said, "The carriage awaits" or something. Nobody gave two monkeys whether I was any good at this line, but for me, it was all I had and I was very, very anxious. I am not actually a very good example. I have this conversation sometimes with people and have sort of given it up because their faces drop and they get very depressed because it sounds terrible – 20 years of feeling like an idiot doing these scary things. I used to see the lollipop lady on the way to work and she would be laughing with the children in the sun and I'm going to rehearsals...

'She was a particularly nice lollipop lady at the end of our road and every time I saw her, my stomach used to turn. I used to wonder, what was I trying to prove? What's the big deal here? What, that you can act? Who gives a shit? You can have a life! I used to do this all the time, but I can't do anything else and I didn't want to be the guy who said I can't do it, but then I got lucky with various people. People helped me so much. And then I surprised myself. I surprised myself little by little and then I have surprised myself a lot and I am forever taking jobs which apparently are out of my range and then turns out that, guess what, they are not actually, even though I say so myself.

'I am not saying I am the world's greatest actor, but I am saying I do the gig. I used to turn down things all the time, like quite big stuff, big stuff, in my world, major classical roles in theatre, I turned down. I had to invent a reason like saying, "I'll leave the Tudor verse to others" – that's a Rex Harrison line, I nicked it – or I'd say it wasn't what I wanted to do at the moment and wanted to concentrate on something else. It was because I was scared. Then I retired from Shakespeare. Not that anyone took a blind bit of notice. I can't do it – I am not really interested in Shakespeare. I am only interested in modern idioms, really – trying to make it sound like you have just thought of it and that you have never spoken it before, that's what I get excited about. Because I had to do everything self-consciously and scared, I found out you could do it.

'I heard two things when I was a kid. One was that Sir Laurence Olivier saying that you had to have one hundred per cent confidence and I thought, "I am out of a job." The other was Rod Steiger, who said you've got to burn to act: "If you don't burn, forget about it." I didn't burn – I famously didn't burn, that was my problem. There was no burning going on. All I wanted to do was not work in a garage like the rest of my family. I didn't want to go to work.

'I was always waiting for the guy to come across the room and say, "Bill, I don't know how this happened, but it's really not working out. We've got this other guy and he can do it." But I am not all together a freak. I do know some people who are household names, who have played this theatre, who have been adorned with every prize we have to offer and they lock themselves in the toilet prior to a performance and say they are never coming out. I know people who routinely vomit every night before they go on. And they are people you would be very, very familiar with…'

By now, Simon Pegg, Nighy's co-star in *Guest House Paradiso*, was directing as well as acting and he cast his fellow actor in his debut feature, *Shaun of the Dead*, which was released on 24 August. Described as a romantic comedy with zombies, it told the story of Shaun (Pegg), an appliance salesman whose life and relationship are going nowhere. He also hates his stepfather Philip (Bill). Much of the action focuses around The Winchester pub. A lot of the other scenes concentrate on an uprising of the 'undead' on the streets of London. Bitten by a zombie, Philip remarks: 'It's alright, I ran it under the cold tap.'

George Romero said the film was an 'absolute blast' – a particularly generous comment considering *Shaun of the Dead* was a spoof of his own *Dawn of the Dead* (1978). Horror writer Stephen King hailed it a cult classic and Quentin Tarantino described it as the 'best movie of the year.' One review said: 'In short, *Shaun of the Dead* is the best British comedy for quite some time. It's intelligent, funny and sufficiently gory to keep horror buffs happy.'

The film earned Pegg and his co-writer Edgar Wright the Best Screenplay award at the 7th Annual British Independent Film Awards. It also won acclaim in some revered circles, not least the United States Conference of Catholic Bishops, who have their own Office of Film and Broadcasting review group. Although the group gave the film a classification of 'O', meaning morally offensive, they said it was 'one of the most subversively funny films to come down the pike in a while' and singled out Bill Nighy for his 'fine performance'.

Bill then moved on to the film of Ian McEwan's novel *Enduring Love*, in which a balloon accident causes deep psychological trauma. Daniel Craig plays Joe, whose relationship with Claire (Samantha Morton) begins to crumble as he tortures himself over the accident and is then stalked by an unhinged Jed (Rhys Ifans). Bill was in the role of Robin, married to Rachel (Susan Lynch). The couple were Joe and Claire's best friends and were created for the film – they did not appear in McEwan's original story – because director Roger Michell wanted 'another version of love in the film, a successful take on married love. I wanted to have a successful North London marriage to run alongside the horrors that Joe and Claire are experiencing and they were able to embody this'. Bill summed up his role alongside Susan as 'there to demonstrate a love that has endured and to show how love can endure.' It was not an addition to the original story that was liked by everyone, with a critic for futuremovies.co.uk commenting: 'The main difficulty some audiences may have with *Enduring Love* is that it is populated almost entirely by cold, unlikeable characters (well, unless you count the wisecracking addition of the ubiquitous Bill Nighy who seems to have wandered in from another movie set)'

Also appearing was Ben Wishaw (Spud), who earlier featured alongside Bill in *Ready When You Are, Mr McGill*. But there was one behind-the-scenes participator for whom the film has special memories. Artist Glenys Barton was called to create a sculpture of Bill's character, which featured in several scenes, and had a sitting with him. She recalls: 'When I came away at the end of the afternoon and set off for my studio my sides ached with laughing and I was a bit worried that the amazing entertainment that I had experienced might have distracted me from the main task. And I felt that perhaps I should have been paid for such an exclusive ticket. Bill is a lovely, friendly guy and he has taken an interest in my work.' Bill would later visit Glenys's exhibition at London's Flowers East Gallery – and kindly ensured it got press coverage.

Enduring Love was released on 26 November and although it did not lead to an award for Bill, it did scoop several at the 2004 British Independent Film Awards, the same year that Simon Pegg and Edgar Wright won best screenplay award for *Shaun of the Dead*.

Samantha Morton won an award for best supporting actress; Daniel Craig for best actor; Roger Michell for best director and cinematographer Haris Zambarloukos for best technical achievement. *Enduring Love* was nominated for best film at the awards ceremony – but lost out to *Vera Drake*, the story of an abortionist (played by Imelda Staunton) in 1950s England which swept the board with six awards including one for Staunton as best actress.

Chapter Seven

The Girl, The Galaxy and the G8

The year 2005 began with one particular accolade for Bill: on 10 January, he was included in the fifteenth edition of *Who's Who*, the big red book that has been a register of Britain's most influential people for 160 years. All Bill's stage and screen work up to that date was listed, together with his recreations of 'reading, rhythm and blues and walking the dog'. His club was listed as The Garrick. Incidentally, he also gets a mention in the film guide *Halliwell's Who's Who*, where he is described as a 'lanky, laconic English actor from the stage...'

Given his past, Bill was a very reasonable choice to voice Dylan – not his childhood and enduring singing hero, but the hippy rabbit – in a feature-length version of *The Magic Roundabout*. He was teamed once more with Jim Broadbent (playing Brian the Snail), plus Kylie Minogue as Florence, Robbie Williams (Dougal), Joanna Lumley (Ermintrude the pink cow) and Richard O'Brien (creator of *The Rocky Horror Show*) as Zebedee.

The Magic Roundabout was originally created for French television by Serge Danot in the mid-1960s, but it went on to win a cult following in Britain in the sixties and seventies, especially among those who thought they read a lot of references to drug use into what was meant to be children's tea-time television. At one point 8 million tuned into the quirky programme, which aired just before the news; voices for the original British version were provided by Eric Thompson, late father of the Oscar-winning actress, Emma Thompson.

Commenting on his invitation to take the role in the full-length feature film, Bill said: 'They were looking for a deranged, stoned-out individual and for some reason they thought of me. I took it as a compliment and Dylan plays no small part in the action side of the movie, which was very satisfying.' It was pleasing, too, to see the reviews that he received for giving a voice to the much-loved rabbit *and* getting to sing the Kinks' Sixties hit, *You Really Got Me*.

In April 2005 came the long-awaited big-screen version of *The Hitchhiker's Guide to the Galaxy* and another chance to work alongside Martin Freeman (who played Arthur Dent). Stephen Fry was the narrator and Kelly Macdonald (one of Bill's co-stars in *State of Play*) took the part of a reporter. The background to the film was somewhat fraught: although Douglas Adams had turned his sci-fi phenomenon into a hit radio and TV series, a five-part trilogy of novels and a BAFTA-winning computer game, he was anxious about it becoming a full-blown movie, saying that it would be like 'trying to grill a steak by having a succession of people blow on it.'

Sadly, after a 20-year battle with Disney to get the film made, Adams was to die of a heart attack. Scripting of the project was handed to Karey Kirkpatrick, who had been involved in *Chicken Run* (2000). Hardened fans were sceptical and Bill himself had never actually seen the earlier TV series or heard the radio serialisation, but he had read the book and had a lot of fun with his role of Slartibartfast – 'I'd rather be happy than right' – the self-effacing planet designer. And when it came to it, he was pleased that he had not seen or heard any earlier versions: 'I'm grateful now that I've come to play the part because it would just complicate things and I have enough trouble as it is. I think I've reached that difficult age when I can only portray men from other dimensions.

'I had plans to play Slartibartfast as a God-like figure with a big, deep voice. One of the embarrassing things you get with older actors, and I hoped it would never happen to me, is that you get a part which says "quite old" – in this case, something like "incredibly elderly" – and you think, "Oh, I'll have to act really old, then." So you go along and go "uurrrrrghhh!" and the director says, "None of that is actually necessary" and you realise you are actually old enough.'

As ever, he was an entertaining interviewee when telling journalists about the role, almost living his screen character as he talked. He told *Time Out*: 'Well, he's God's architect, or he's got God's phone number, or something. The whole central joke about *Hitchhiker's*, as you will have noticed, is that you get these extraordinary things happening with extraordinary people in extraordinary places, but they react to it in a regular and normal fashion. I take Martin on this huge intergalactic trip and show him all these things, the likes of which you can't even imagine, and I do it as if I'm showing him around the office. Which is, in fact, what I'm doing because it's the factory floor. And Arthur is required to go on this incredible journey, whilst moaning about how he can't get a decent cup of tea, or he wants a pint of lager or something. That's part of what I think people mean when they say "Englishness", you know, because we're a whiney, moaning bunch.'

So, what appealed to him most about the part? 'I was aware that Slartibartfast had the grooviest, longest, stupidest name in the film and I was obscurely proud of that.' And he also liked the feeling of power that playing one of God's right-hand men gave him: 'It feels pretty good. If somebody's casting God, or the next best thing, and they think of you, I think you have to be grateful. And once I learnt how to pronounce my name, it was great. For the first two weeks, I was quite confident. I was calling myself Bartifastblart and I thought that was pretty good, but somebody then pointed out that, actually, it was the other way around.'

But he did have some ideas about how he would rule the world if he had Slartibartfast's God-like abilities.

He told *BBC Film*: 'The buildings would be French-inspired, they would be château-like, and I would live in the biggest one, and I would live on a hill, and my name would be King Bill. And my name wouldn't be Slartibartfast, I would live in a big place, where people would worship me and the Rolling Stones were the house band and they had to live in the basement until I said so, until they came up, usually on Friday night, when they entertained me and my friends. ...I am devoted to them. I have never completely recovered from what happens when Keith [Richards] hits the strings and Charlie [Watts] kicks in. Very few things move me to patriotism and the Rolling Stones are one of them. They are just the greatest rhythm and blues band in the world. And I'd have Aretha Franklin come to dinner...'

The movie received good reviews with Bill (and Fry) once again singled out. A review on Myvillage.com commented: 'The essential Britishness of the film is provided by the delectable Stephen Fry and Bill Nighy, who are more English than chips, awkward dinner parties and halitosis. Who better to voice The Guide, a book which contains all the knowledge in the universe, than bulging-brained Fry, who uses the perfect amount of middle-class haughtiness, irony and intelligence to narrate the delightfully complicated story. And Nighy can't fail as planet builder Slartibartfast (who, as every nerd knows, won an award for creating the twiddly bits around Norwegian fjords) because he based the world-weary alien on the nation's best-loved character, Bill Nighy.'

Another reviewer, Sean Nelson, while not warming completely to the film, did comment: 'Still, whenever there are at least two British actors on-screen – especially Martin Freeman or the film-stealing Bill Nighy...' The *Scotsman*'s film critic wrote: 'Cast as the eccentric planet builder Slartibartfast – who won an award for Norway! – he's like an adrenaline shot to the heart and jolts the film back to life.'

The Hitchhiker's Guide to the Galaxy was released on 29 April 2005 and went on to scoop a not-unacceptable £50 million worldwide. Bill had just one small regret about the film: he did not get to keep the fur coat that Slartibartfast strutted around in, the coat that women everywhere told him they wanted off his back, 'Which is kind of nice, makes me feel good.'

The Girl in the Café – first seen on screen on 25 June 2005 – meant a happy reunion for him with its writer Richard Curtis and co-star Kelly Macdonald. Bill plays Lawrence, an unassuming British civil servant and delegate at a G8 summit in Iceland. Lawrence is drawn to Gina (Macdonald), whom he meets in a café, and they attend the summit together – 'Well, it was lovely, sitting directly opposite you. I'm Lawrence, by the way... Don't think because I am not saying much that I wouldn't like to say a lot.'

They then have to deal with crucial decisions, both on a personal and global level. Bill was given a gem of a chat-up line when he first meets Gina: 'Well, don't worry – some of the dullest people in the world are in this room. They are gold medallists in the boredom

Olympics. Anything you say will be more interesting than anything they have ever said.' A later scene has him talking about a dream he had, along the usual lines, of the Rolling Stones begging him for a job: 'Mick Jagger and Ronnie Wood are together on speakerphone pleading with me to inject a bit of new blood into the band... or Keith Richards is handing me his guitar and saying, "Come on, man, you have the music – play. We'll give you as much heroin as you like, just lend us your hot licks."'

Of the project, he said: 'I read the script and it took me about three seconds to heartily agree to be involved. The script is a cracker, as you'd expect from Richard Curtis, who is kind of world-class in this area. It's extremely funny, I hope. Otherwise, I'm going to kill myself. And it's romantic, as you'd also expect. Uh, again, if it's not I'll have to kill myself. But I'm assured that it's going OK. It's also, I hope, quite affecting and touching and moving. But I had no hesitation in being involved.

'It's a wonderful part. It's a part that I haven't been asked to play recently in as much as I play a rather reserved gentleman. Meek is how he's described. He's kind of pathologically shy, as a result of which he's led a kind of lonesome existence, and within the course of the film, the sky clears for a moment and he's joined in a rather unlikely fashion by an extremely wonderful and glamorous young lady. And it has a fun, profound effect upon him which, hopefully, will be amusing, too.'

He admitted it was an unusual story in terms of a

romantic lead because of the age difference between the two main characters, but added: 'It's very close to my heart; it's one of my favourite jobs of all time. I love to work with Richard Curtis, because that was my second time and I think it was a great achievement of his to integrate the information and social message [about world poverty] that he wished to deliver so successfully into a romantic comedy movie. And to work with Kelly Macdonald was thrilling and wonderful, because she's a rare and beautiful talent. She and I, we relished that film, playing that job. You felt that you were involved in something which might, even to the tiniest degree, help with a very serious situation. Yeah, it was a gas.

'So, I mean, as a romantic hero, well, come on! Nobody laughed. I mean, probably my friends did. The guys I know probably went, "Come on!" And, especially some younger women, I'm sure went, "Are you serious?" But most people didn't laugh. Hardly a day goes by when somebody doesn't come up to me in the street and say, "You made such a lovely couple. Did you get things together at the end?" And I'd say, "Well, I don't know – I like to think so." So, that was a great opportunity given to me by Richard, which I'm very grateful for. It was a beautiful script and every single word was there on the page. One of the benefits of my job now is that I don't ever again have to work with writers who need any kind of help.'

He described his character as 'an average mess isolated by self-consciousness. He finds it almost impossibly difficult to present himself to people. As for the romantic arena, you figure there has been little or no activity there at all. When he meets the girl in the café they have a kind of accidental conversation and then he scares himself by perhaps for the first time asking a girl out to lunch and she scares him even more by saying "yes".'

As well as the romantic elements, the role called for him to deliver statistics about poverty, while maintaining a character almost disabled by a sense of inadequacy. Lawrence does eventually declare himself, which although liberating for his character, was intimidating for Bill: 'It was the bit you fear the most. Where you feel, "Oh, please God, oh God, please let me get that bit right! Don't let me interfere with the news, let me deliver this as cleanly as possible."'

One of his most magical moments was during filming in Iceland: 'I stood at a chain link fence and watched an aeroplane disappear into the Icelandic sky and then you curse from the bottom of your boots that your heart is now in exile. It was as near as I'll get to Casablanca.'

The project was not just a professional challenge but a vehicle to publicise his involvement in lobbying G8 members and the whole issue of lack of overseas aid to developing countries. Certainly, when he appeared on the BBC that June, he had researched the situation and put forward forceful arguments: 'At the summit in July, eight men in one room could literally save hundreds of millions of lives. Currently a child dies completely unnecessarily every three seconds: 30,000 children die every day, so it is an emergency. I have been alerted to the facts. I didn't know that in the time it takes you to click your fingers, a child will die. But I don't want people to think that after seeing this film they have to say their prayers or that we want their money. Nobody wants your credit card number, you don't reach for the phone at the end of the show, you just kick back and watch what, hopefully, is a legitimate piece of light entertainment, romantic comedy. It's built for laughs... You could remain blissfully unaware of any other purpose the film might have. We are not trying to get anyone's attention under false pretences.'

Though nominated for a Golden Globe Award for *The Girl in the Café*, sadly he did not go on to win. But he was deeply grateful, both for the recognition and for the chance to play such a thoughtful role: 'Obviously there is a message and do you feel any kind of responsibility or any pressure because of that? I laugh because yes, I do. I do feel a unique responsibility and a unique degree of pressure because you want very passionately to get it right. I didn't sleep for the first week, but then I often don't sleep for the first week. In this case, I suppose it was twice as bad. But the expectation therefore is quite high and when the expectation is high, the pressure is great. But mostly the pressure is not to mess it up because you want it to deliver in a way that you don't normally want moves to deliver. You want this one to deliver one thousand per cent.'

The Girl in the Café certainly delivered as far as the critics were concerned: 'The film is graced by two truthful and magical central performances from Bill Nighy and Kelly Macdonald, and, thanks to Curtis's dialogue, it is just as funny as *Love Actually* or *Four Weddings and a Funeral*,' wrote the *Telegraph*. Timesonline.co.uk said: 'Bill Nighy, reprising the Hugh Grant hapless male role, only with more "umms" and less hair, was engaging as a shy British Treasury official.'

Although he might have been surprised at such a favourable reaction to *The Girl in the Café*, his good friend Richard Curtis certainly wasn't: 'Bill is completely delightful and wonderfully self-effacing. The words that come up most in his work are "that was crap" and "f*** up". When I texted him the other day to say that *Girl in the Café* had gone down well in a screening, instead of replying "Bravo!" he simply texted that he was glad he hadn't f***** up totally.'

Curtis describes Bill's acting technique – although of course, he himself would say he doesn't actually have a technique – as 'heightened truthfulness; a performance that seems natural, but is underpinned by precision comic timing. Bill is a perfect example of this in *Love Actually*: one hundred per cent true and then 100 per cent funny, when necessary. And in *Girl in the Café* he really showed his full range – funny, immensely moving and immensely serious. But I also like the fact that his performances are slightly larger than life – while not appearing to be so. He has certain magnificence.'

The Girl in the Café went on to win three Emmy Awards: for Best TV Movie and Best Writing in the mini-series/TV movie category. Kelly Macdonald won Best Supporting Actress in a mini-series. There was some speculation among fans as to why Bill was not an award-winner. The *Chicago Tribune* commented: 'Sometimes even when the Emmys get it right, they still get it wrong. Witness Kelly Macdonald's win for *The Girl in the Café* – the problem is not that she won, it's that she wasn't actually playing a supporting role. The HBO film was really a two-person vehicle for Macdonald and the tremendous Bill Nighy.'

There was some suggestion that he lost out because of new Emmy rules that year, under which actors considered for one of the awards must put their name down for a particular film they wish to be nominated for, with Bill choosing *Gideon's Daughter* (2005) over *The Girl in the Café*. But the work gave him one of his first tastes of stardom, with fans still coming up to offer their congratulations, a year or so later. 'I have been approached more at airports and dinner parties than anything else I've done in a long time. I think *The Girl in the Café* tends to linger in people's minds,' he remarked.

Following this, he was to use his distinctive and compelling voice in a very different project, narrating on *Meerkat Manor* on the Discovery Animal Planet Channel. *Meerkat Manor* was described as a soap opera with a difference: taking one group of the 12-inch burrowing animals living in the Kalahari Desert and following their everyday life: 'They're very charismatic animals and have all been given names. It's a bit like meerkat soap – you have to tune in next week to find out who's got pregnant, etc. It's been researched by Cambridge scientists and is rather good.'

With success following success, he appeared in *The Constant Gardener*, which was released on 31 August 2005. It was his first John le Carré project since *The Little Drummer Girl*, 21 years before. Ralph Fiennes plays a junior diplomat, who falls for fiery activist Rachel Weisz and is subsequently drawn into a web of conspiracy and murder. Bill took the part of Sir Bernard Pellegrin, a member of the British High Commission.

The plot centres on a remote area of Northern Kenya, where activist Tessa Quayle (Weisz) is brutally murdered. Pellegrin (Bill) is suave and deeply sinister while Justin Quayle (Fiennes) seeks to uncover a plot in which drug companies and governments are exploiting HIV-positive Africans. Weisz won an Oscar for her role.

Ever grateful for the meaty parts he was being offered, Bill said he was delighted to play a 'nobby toff', adding, 'I don't come from that background at all, so it's very nice to be playing an upper middle-class Englishman.'

The critics loved his rather menacing 'nobby toff': 'If ever a face was made for villainy, it's Bill Nighy's. His decadently long jaw and narrow, sneaky eyes serve him well as an oily politician. Nighy is like a coiled snake as he watches Fiennes' mild-mannered hero put together the mystery. He gives the kind of slow-burn, slime-and-smile performance that actors like Claude Rains and Robert Shaw used to give in classic supporting roles, and he stands out for his lack of scenery-chewing,' wrote the *New York Daily News*.

Timesonline.co.uk said: 'And Bill Nighy is fabulously insincere as the minister who tries to pin the murder on an infatuated doctor. "Albert is homosexual," says Justin. "Well, I've known one or two savage queens in my time," quips Nighy.'

He was nominated for a British Independent Film Award for Best Supporting Actor for his role as Sir Bernard Pellegrin. In fact, *The Constant Gardener* was the night's big winner, taking the BIFA awards for Best Film, Best Actor (Ralph Fiennes) and Best Actress (Rachel Weisz).

It had been another successful year for Bill, but personally, 2005 was to end on a rather lonely note. That Christmas and New Year, he stayed at home while Diana and their daughter Mary travelled to India so that Diana could re-trace her great-grandmother's flight from marauding mutineers across what used to be known as the Central Provinces. Before becoming a policeman, her great-grandfather served 23 years in the army in India and her great-grandmother was forced to flee from the Indian Mutiny after her father was killed. The trip formed part of the years of research that Diana had been carrying out into her father's family life, and which would later culminate in a book.

Bill used his quiet time at home to prepare for another hectic year.

Chapter Eight

Sex, Sea-legs and Scandal

Bill's next project was *Gideon's Daughter* for the BBC which was shown on February 26th, 2006. It meant a reunion with Stephen Poliakoff and co-star Miranda Richardson, and saw him in the role of PR chief Gideon Warner, helping the government deal with the death of the Princess of Wales and prepare for the Millennium, while desperately trying to come to terms with his daughter slipping away from him. His character is eventually saved when he meets Stella (Richardson), who is coming to terms with the death of her own son.

Bill couldn't wait to grab the part: 'Oh man, the script was just great! I read and completely loved it. I picked up the phone immediately and said, "I'd like to be in this, please!" I had zero hesitation.' He had empathy with his role because in some ways it mirrored his own situation. 'Gideon is someone I feel I understand,' he revealed. 'He is a man who is finding it increasingly difficult to pay attention at work and yet the less he listens, the more successful he becomes. When you don't care, people give you everything. If you can arrange not to want stuff, people hand it to you for free. That's a great joke! Gideon has worked hard over the years and been very successful, but guess what? It didn't work. Part of the human condition is that we all go around saying, "When I get that bit of my life straight, I can pull over and relax. If I can only get that person to love me or get that perfect pair of shoes, then I'll be sorted. But guess what? You get the shoes and nothing changes. Now you can't find the right handbag to go with it. When you've attained one thing, there is always something else tantalisingly dangling at the end of the stick that you need. That's a universal experience.'

Gideon's Daughter was a new departure for him. He was instructed by Poliakoff to cut back on his physical performance and concentrate on delivering the lines. The director asked Bill not to blink so much – in fact, not to move so much generally, as he usually does. Bill was a little bemused by this. He told aintitcool.com: 'Part of it is that I think that if it's just me turning up, then everyone will go to sleep, so I think I have to do something in order to earn my keep, you know what I mean? In other words, it's born of certain insecurity, I suppose, about my general physical presence, that it's not substantial enough on its own, which I'm working on, maybe for other roles. Steven put a stop to all of that – you know, this is not going to be any of the stuff that you've done... forget all the stuff you've done before. I want you to be very still, and it was challenging.

'For the first couple of weeks, I kept having to go up to him after takes and say, are you sure? Because it was just me standing there trying to be still, trying to tell the story as best I could without dramatising it, physically. It was very unsettling for me, because it's not what I naturally do. I can't do the stuff suggested in drama school – re-creating the emotional state the character was in. I've tried, but I can't; I have no method. What I naturally do is, I've always done it since I've been on stage, I do tend to use movement... it's not necessarily a conscious decision at the beginning, it just happens when I'm in the fire. Opening plays is the scariest thing I've ever done, just about. Therefore, stuff happens. In me, it's reflected in a sort of physicality. And I then get to pick whether I want to hang on to those things or not, when I'm in sober reflection. Do you know what I mean? Because with the theatre you're doing it over and over again: it seems to me to be a way of trying to suggest, as you would with your face before a camera, what's happening to your character internally.

'So, you indicate with your body. You tell the story a touch more physically than perhaps other actors might, I don't know. And sometimes, I don't do that. Sometimes, there are roles where you think, your job here is to not get in the way and just try to be as simple as possible. There was a time when you were supposed to question everything the director said, to create some kind of conflict, out of which creativity would be borne. But I love it when they tell you what to do, you know: "Start there, walk over there, say the line and I'll shout: 'Cut!'" I think it's groovy.

'When we were filming with Stephen Poliakoff, his first note to me – he prefaced it with, "That was marvellous", which is always a good start – anyway, his note was: "Don't wiggle your eyes about so much," and you know, my heart leapt – because I know that. I know how to not make my eyes wiggle about.'

Sometimes it's hard to understand that Bill actually loves what he does, that despite the lack of faith in his own talent, he is deeply passionate about any project he undertakes: 'I have become more and more interested. And I am very grateful for that because I think that sometimes the opposite is true. My enthusiasm for it has grown and continues to grow. I think it is a very, very wonderful job and a hard job. There are harder jobs, obviously, and I try and remind myself of that, but the thing you have to achieve, the simple things, like – for instance – trying to say a line as if it has just occurred to you, which technically is something I find endlessly fascinating, I don't think I will ever get to the end of that. I don't think anyone ever does. And the idea that you have to look as if everything that has happened is just occurring to you, and the technique of trying to sell that to an audience, whether it is in front of a camera or in front of an audience, is something I continue to be fascinated by.'

The project was equally satisfying for Miranda Richardson, who describes Bill as a 'complete gent', who is, 'complex and *simpatico*, which is a lovely combination. And he plays great music. You always hear the Rolling Stones coming out of his trailer. What more could you want?'

He won a Golden Globe for the role. His acceptance speech was one of humility (and humour), as might be expected: 'Thank you very much. I'd like to thank everybody for this… it seems too crazy to me. But I used to think that prizes were damaging and divisive until I got one. And now they seem sort of meaningful and real. I'd like to thank everybody involved in *Gideon's Daughter* – it was a big deal for me. I'd like to thank Miss Emily Blunt, who you've already honoured this evening. I'd particularly like to thank Miss Miranda Richardson, who starred in the film, who is, as you don't need me to tell you, one of the most wonderful actresses currently operating in the world. And I thank her. A big hand for Miranda, please. And I'd like to thank Stephen Poliakoff, the man who wrote and directed the film. He is the most remarkable writer and the most wonderful director. I've worked with him on several occasions; it's a great honour and I am very proud to be associated with the show. And I accept this award on his behalf and on behalf of BBC America. Thank you, everybody, big up.'

He admitted that he never expected to win: 'It was a genuine shock, really. I walked literally speechless to the microphone. It was a wonderful thing and I was very proud for the show, because it's dear to my heart.'

It was a wonderful moment for Bill who, at the start of his career, never considered that he would reach the stage where he would be given any kind of award. In fact, even in the middle stages, he never believed that he would stand on a stage to give thanks for recognition: 'I never included myself in that group of people that might get prizes. It wasn't like now that prizes are everywhere. No, I never rehearsed a speech in front of the mirror, I never thought I'd get a prize, and I was right. I mean, for 30 years I was absolutely spot-on. I was correct, I wasn't mistaken. It happened relatively recently that I got prizes and then I would absolutely not rehearse in front of the mirror. I mainly wind up in front of a microphone with nothing to say. And then I have to think of something quickly, because it's too scary to think it beforehand. You just put things off, you know, if they're scary. It's standard procrastination. I didn't think I'd ever be a prize-winning actor.'

No doubt he felt he deserved the award for breaking one of his golden rules – taking his clothes off. Make that *two* of his golden rules as he had a sex scene too. 'I did have to take my top off. It was a lonely moment, I can tell you,' he recalled. His bedfellow was Ronni Ancona, who played Gideon's girlfriend, Barbara. 'I had to lie on top of a naked Ronni... Had to simulate passion with noises. You wake up and think, "Ah, what am I doing today? Oh yes, today I have to simulate passion with noises." It's never a good start to the day. It's very exposing to make noises because you never know what noises other people make. It's bonkers, ludicrous. The only way to get through it is to think that your job is to look after the girl. That is your responsibility – protect her from the crew, obscure parts of her body. The trouble is, you end up in positions from which it is impossible to make *lurve*. But playing the gentleman helps take your mind off your own predicament, off your puny body and your non-existent genitalia. Having someone making up your bum with half a dozen sparks watching is not my idea of eroticism. Oh man! And it's always so unnecessary. There is never a justification for it in the plot. It is all to do with budget and having a chance to show breasts.'

Indeed, it could have been very awkward for Ronni as well. She bemoaned the fact that she was meant to be a 'skinny bird' but was in fact four months' pregnant when filming began.

Hopefully, Bill thought the embarrassment of the situation was worth it.

Bill appeared in flashback in a sequel to *Underworld* – *Underworld Evolution* – where he is revealed to be the treacherous murderer of Kate Beckinsale's parents. He then threw himself into the incredibly fun – but highly unrecognisable – role of Davy Jones in *Dead Man's Chest*, the second in the series of *Pirates of the Caribbean* films, directed by Gore Verbinski. The appearance saw him star once more alongside Tom Hollander and Keira Knightley, as well as Jonathan Pryce and Johnny Depp. Somewhere, amid the gloop and tentacles, he was there.

Unlike his vampire creation in *Underworld*, after which he vowed, 'Nobody would ever be allowed to do anything of that kind to me again,' fortunately he did not have to spend hours in a makeup department being transformed into the marine monstrosity with an accent 'with a Scottish spin' that sounded like it had a permanent heavy cold. Much to his great relief, this was computer-generated. He confessed: 'Oh it's all CGI! My face is made up to bleed into the creature and I have to wear those funky computer pyjama trousers and have white dots all over the place for the mapping points for the computer. My fear was that even if the creature was successful, it would look like it was in a different dimension than the real people. The first time I got any of the images, I was photographing and texting them on the phone, just sending them home to creep people out.'

He managed to see the funny side of being the one on set wearing trainers with bobbles on them and having to stand alongside the likes of Johnny Depp: 'I'm the only guy wearing this and then they show you this picture of this incredibly fantastic, the most dangerous and terrifying thing on the ocean waves, and then they say, "Act!" Short of putting a sack over your head or putting a chain around your ankle, it's like being given a serious handicap. Then, between Gore Verbinski and myself, we came up with a way of doing it. I was amazed when I saw the creature because it had evolved from the pictures I was originally shown. They were pretty much the same, but it was much more beautiful.

'It was brilliantly achieved and all those stupid things I did on the set, trying to be scary and weird, they actually had translated them onto the creature. They always said they were going to do that and I know they meant well, but I didn't think it was possible and in fact, they pulled it off.'

He took all the teasing in his stride, too: 'People would just look at you, say "Hi" and then they'd look away. The crew were ashamed on your behalf and then, after you've been around for a few days, then the jokes would start and then the jokes ran out after about the second week. Then it's completely normal that you're standing there, talking to a man with dots all over his face. It's only every now and again when someone takes a photograph that you realise that you look incredibly lame...

'There was a good day also, because I had a crew that also had to look similarly stupid, so there was a day when I walked around the corner of the set and I saw six other guys dressed like me and I nearly kissed them. It was such a big day.'

Not that it mattered to the hordes of film-goers, but he loved to detail the somewhat 'foggy' origins of Davy Jones, a one-time captain on the Ship of Death, who is 'not sure if that's real anymore. He suffers profoundly. And he's lived under the sea for so long he's been effectively transformed into a half-squid creature. Exactly why he was vanquished to the bottom of the sea, we can't say, but his desire to protect anything relating to his treasure has no bounds.' In short, laughed a delighted Bill: 'His job in the movie is largely to put the fear of death into people and the only time in your life you will ever see Davy Jones or indeed his terrible crew on the horror ship is at the point of death...'

It was, of course, a ridiculous role, but another Bill Nighy scene-stealer: 'It wasn't what you call naturalism because you can't claim I'm over the top because, you know, I'm a squid. And I rule the waves...' He needed some humour to cope with the role, which included spending 10 weeks under a rain machine, but he was deeply touched when, at the end of filming, both cast and crew presented him with a personalised present – a squid cake the size of a coffee table with a picture of his Davy Jones on top! There was a particular expression of affection from his co-star Kate Beckinsale who said: 'Sadly, he's not in it as much as he was. We'd visit him a bit and that was very nice. He's just a kind of rock-star god to us. We were sorry to see him go so quickly. We sliced his head in half last time. If we had only known he was going to be so cool, we wouldn't have done that...'

Being half-crab, half-squid was challenging in other ways, too. Bill has the proud acting boast of having played three different 'undead' characters: a zombie in *Shaun of the Dead*, a vampire in the *Underworld* series and of course, Davy Jones.

While filming for *Dead Man's Chest* was taking place, so too were some scenes for the follow-up, *Pirates of the Caribbean: At World's End* (2007). 'It was an incredible undertaking,' he recalled. 'And Gore handled it so well. His attention to details is remarkable, from the rings on your fingers to the design on the curtains. Nothing escapes him.'

Pirates meant a gruelling schedule, with most of his working year accounted for, although in a not unpleasant way, as he got to see Granada and the Bahamas. Despite the latter part of the year being taken up with his Davy Jones role, incredibly he managed to find the time, 'for other movies in between.'

Back at his hotel, he kept sane with an iPod full of his old friends, Bob Dylan and the Stones, during non-working periods ('I respond very well to the hotel experience') and watched the occasional football match on TV. That, and a diet of fresh fish put him in 'heaven' throughout filming. He did not have the company of long-term partner, Diana Quick, at any point during the long stint, though – she was touring in a stage play and then took to the West End.

Some critics said they felt cheated at not seeing their hero's face in *Pirates*. Others had no idea who was playing Davy Jones until the credits rolled, but most simply heaped on the praise. 'Jones himself is a flawless creation, all dripping tentacles and twitching mannerisms, complemented effectively by Bill Nighy's harsh Hibernian whisper,' commented screen magazine, *Empire*. 'Nighy does a great job of getting across his tormented character despite his face being hidden behind special effects,' stated the *Hollywood Reporter*. *Variety* magazine's film critic wrote: 'Best of all is Davy himself, whose remarkable visage is festooned with a beard of moving octopus tentacles and whose strength as a singular villain is heightened by Nighy's wily performance.'

Pirates of the Caribbean: Dead Man's Chest was released on 7 July 2006 and broke box-office records, taking $132m in America in just three days, beating the previous high of £115m achieved by *Spider-Man* in 2002. On the first Friday of its release, it took $55.5m, beating the previous record-holder, *Star Wars Episode III: Revenge of the Sith* (2005). Worldwide, it raked in $1,06,659,812. Sadly, one country that would not experience the delight of Bill as Davy Jones – or indeed any of his co-stars – was China, which refused to screen the film because of its 'violent and supernatural content'. The government-controlled Film Bureau didn't approve of the portrayal of the 'souls of the dead or the ferocious octopus-faced character of Davy Jones. But then, China only passes 20 foreign films a year.

Bill was astute enough to believe that the film might just be a success and in true Nighy altruistic style, he turned his view to charitable advantage. He hung onto his original script, complete with doodles and comments to himself, and in March 2007 donated it to raise funds for another of his worthy causes – High Tide, a new writing theatre festival aimed at supporting the work of young writers. Bill is patron of the festival, which premièred eight new plays that Easter weekend at The Cut, in Halesworth, Suffolk. He has a country retreat in Suffolk, not far from his great friend, Richard Curtis.

Bill was to become a regular on BBC7 radio. One of his first appearances was in June of that year in *The Medical Detectives*. It was a series of dramas based on real-life medical disasters, including an outbreak of cholera in London's Soho in 1854, yellow fever in 19th-century Cuba, a bizarre epidemic among the middle-class inhabitants of an Essex suburb and mysterious deaths in the Arctic. The series starred Nicky Henson from the BBC's *EastEnders* soap, Peter Capaldi, Ken Stott and Clive Merrison. Bill appeared in one of the episodes – 'Tune in, cop out and get Nighy,' declared one fanzine.

Behind the scenes, he accepted a very special private role. In August 2006, he agreed to become an ambassador for the charity organisation DebRA. The organisation had come to the fore following a television programme called *The Boy Whose Skin Fell Off* and aims to support those with the genetic skin-blistering condition Epidermolysis Bullosa (EB).

His other big movie of 2006 was *Notes on a Scandal*, based on Zoe Heller's novel, starring Judi Dench and Cate Blanchett and directed by Richard Eyre (*Skylight*). Bill was delighted to be working with him again: 'He's incredibly bright, that's what you want from a director; you want somebody cleverer than you. That's what I always hope for. I've been very, very lucky. He has the thing that I lack, which is that I can do my bit – I'm not good at an overview of any kind.

'I have a couple of bad habits. One is that I always want to play the end because I can't bear the suspense – I always want to indicate to the audience that I'm a really nice guy, which may or may not be part of the gig. My other bad habit is that I always try to sell things as if I'm trying to sell a lie. Richard also has great taste and a great bullshit detector. Whenever I wanted to sell it like some kind of salesperson, trying to do something that was other than be authentically there, he was very good at politely suggesting that I stop that. He is very good at tuning your performance. I think he did a little bit of acting in his university days. Sometimes, that helps a great deal. It doesn't matter if you're particularly good at it or not, just the fact that you ever attempted it does really help when you're trying to communicate something to an actor. He's extremely good on the text and how to get the most value out of the nuances.'

In fact, the two had a mutual respect. Director Richard Eyre said of Bill: 'He is one of those actors who has got better with time: when he was young, he was a very attractive, beguiling man, but now he has a kind of diffidence, a kind of droll stance of looking at the world, which as a young man made him seem a little lightweight. The older Bill gets, the more attractive he becomes, and the more that diffidence, drollness, seems like a mature wisdom.'

Dame Judi Dench played Barbara Covett, a somewhat predatory lesbian teacher, who becomes obsessed with young art teacher Sheba Hart (Cate

Blanchett). Bill played Richard, the Sheba's older husband, who is crushed by her unfaithfulness – not with the spinster teacher, but with a young pupil – 'Are you insane? If you meant to destroy us, why not do it with an adult? That's the convention!' The family was already under pressure caring for a son suffering with Downs Syndrome. For Bill, this was a powerful role and one that also allowed him some humour and pithiness – 'I'm not saying I was so fucking fabulous, but I was here.' After Davy Jones, we actually got to see his face, too.

Talking about *Notes on a Scandal*, he told *NYC Movie Guru*: 'It was bit of a holiday, actually; it was a relief. It was very nice to play a regular human being, having played zombies and vampires and squids. It was also nice to play somebody who was, broadly speaking, in reasonable shape until events overcome him. He was somebody who was, sort of, a good thing in the world. My job wasn't to indicate how damaged he was, or what kind of a nuisance he might turn out to be. He was just a regular guy with a family and it was nice doing family stuff and being a dad.'

But he did not do any research for the role of Richard – 'I never seem to get around to it,' he observed, adding, 'If the script is any good, it's in there... You just try to deliver the role without moral judgment because that's not my business... the writing helps enormously – it doesn't need any help from me. I really did enjoy the environment they gave us. They gave us a very witty, very accurate set – a representation of a very upper middle-class English environment, where you have the passport in the fruit bowl, which always made me feel very uneasy. I wanted to put it somewhere safe, but that was a very witty touch. That's the kind of household we have. I think it's referred to as shabby chic.'

But the role enabled him to reach deep into the heart of a husband who has been made a fool of: 'When we shot the scene where I confront her with the affair, I hit a level of anger I'm not accustomed to reaching for.' He admits it was a hard scenario to film: 'That was a big day at the office; that was tough and gruelling. I'm not one for complaining that I take it home – I generally come home and have a cup of coffee – but that was a day where I was required to stay very unhappy and very, very angry for a very long time.'

It was also a highly notable scene with one reviewer commenting: 'Then comes the moment when he learns his schoolteacher wife is having an affair with an underage student, and his reaction is so wounded and so real and so explosive that it's almost painful to watch. This is great acting.'

Bill couldn't believe that his screen wife was to be the beautiful Cate Blanchett, confessing he thought it was an April Fool's joke when he was told: 'But it was thrilling because I admire her as much as any actor working.' Then there was Judi Dench, with whom he was working for a third time. He describes her as 'otherworldly in terms of talent and she's a wonderful person and extremely good company, as was Cate. We had a very grim tale to tell, and I think sometimes the equation is that the more scary the story, the more fun you have on the set. I mean, it's not always the case, obviously, but I think in some cases that's the dynamic, and we did have a laugh.' His frustrated and angry character hit home with the critics: *Rolling Stone* described him as 'The ever-amazing Bill Nighy', while *NY* magazine said his performance was 'delightful'.

One bonus was the Belsize Park location of *Notes on a Scandal*. It was literally around the corner from his house in Kentish Town, north London. 'I could have walked to work. I think I did in one case, so that was nice,' he said.

Later, he joined in a campaign over one of his local streets: Little Green Street, off Highgate Road, Kentish Town. Little Green is one of the oldest streets in London and locals objected to it being used as an access road for developers building on derelict land behind it. There were also plans to change the look of it. 'They can't do that, it's senseless,' said Bill.

(Unfortunately all the protestors' efforts were in vain and the Planning Inspectorate later determined that Little Green Street could be used as a truck route).

Notes on a Scandal opened on 27 December 2006. It wasn't one of Bill's most successful films, despite his fine performance, but it did go on to gross nearly $50,000,000 worldwide.

Meanwhile, Diana was busy with her own projects. She had been doing theatre work and then came her first television appearance since *Brideshead Revisited*,

25 years earlier. Diana had taken 19 years out from her acting career to raise daughter Mary, something she described as her 'greatest achievement'. In 2006 she appeared in the BBC2 sitcom *Sensitive Skin* as a sexy sixty-something woman with a lover half her age. Diana welcomed the 'fun role', but said that such a relationship was not something she would ever consider in real life: 'I have lots of male friends who are much younger than me, but I have never met anybody younger, where I've felt we could be kindred spirits. I have never even had an affair with somebody younger than me. I think the sex would be complicated. I would feel quite weird, sexually, with a younger man.'

Bill was happy with the way his working life had gone that year – good roles, good reviews, maybe even for the self-doubting actor, good feelings too: 'It's like I won a competition this year, and this is the prize. To go to work every day with three of the greatest actresses currently operating in the world is identifiable as a pretty good gig. I think these are very specific stories, women who need a significantly older man, and happily they sometimes think of me,' he said of his co-stars who, to his consternation, had helped transform him into what he called, 'the thinking woman's crumpet.' As mentioned previously, he considers himself to be more 'the *drinking* woman's crumpet...'

At the end of 2006, he made a hugely successful and significant return to the stage when he rejoined David Hare for *The Vertical Hour*, which opened on

November 30th at the Music Box Theatre in New York. Directed by Sam Mendes and co-starring Julianne Moore and young actor Andrew Scott, the play saw Bill as reclusive doctor Oliver Lucas, living in Shropshire and hostile to the Iraq war but also expounding wittily on fathers and sons, the sixties, sex and medicine. The storyline really begins with the arrival, from the States, of Lucas's son with his girlfriend, a war correspondent turned Yale political science professor. Old roué Lucas has more than an intellectual interest in his young female visitor.

Despite its theme, *The Vertical Hour* had humour too, which came as a surprise to the audience, but its elements were to prove a winning combination and a special lure to Bill: 'It's about personal relationships and about how half the world is disadvantaged. At the end of the play, you are not solely concerned about where you stand on Iraq – you are concerned about something bigger than that. It's about compassion...' There was one particular line delivered by him, referring to Iraq, which almost invariably was greeted by applause: 'When I knew who the surgeon was going to be, I had a fair idea of what the operation would look like.'

Said Bill: 'I guessed they agreed with the line. I think people were very, very grateful to have these things discussed; it was a very timely thing. We got lucky with the timing. It was very beautifully placed in America, in New York at that time. Both sides of the argument are beautifully expressed. It's about personal relationships and how one's personal responsibility can bleed into the public responsibility and what to do about the fact that most of the world is disadvantaged.... But it's not some exam you have to sit. By the end of the play, hopefully, if we have delivered it properly, you are no longer concerned about where you stand on Iraq solely – you are concerned with something bigger than that. It's about humanity and compassion. It's also very carefully built by David and Sam to have several hundred people laugh uproariously...'

Recalled Mendes: 'The moment I read it, I said to David [Hare] "It's Bill, isn't it?" And he said, "Is it that obvious?" I think the difficult aspect of the part is that there's an element of this man – a lot of anger, a lot of self-righteousness – that Bill does not display in life. He's playing outside of himself in a large part. But this is the thing with Bill: he has lived. He has fought demons in his life and he brings that incredible wealth of self-knowledge onto the stage with him.

'He's walking an incredible tightrope. He is touched with genius and there were a lot of times at rehearsals when I would just watch. There were a couple of occasions I went home to my wife and said that Bill had done some of the best acting I had ever seen. I couldn't quite work out how he was doing it. He walks this extreme tightrope between mannerism and something utterly truthful and completely real, and it is never the same twice. Something comes out different every time, every line is different. It is rhythmical like water. He'll split sentences in odd ways and stress words in strange ways, but somehow it has a feeling of rightness. It's like watching a great jazz player with the confidence to improvise. He moves in a different way every night, so you can never predict it; he doesn't really know where he's going to go, and he does that with the words, too. He'll break a sentence, pause in the most extravagant way, and yet never lose the tune.'

The comments gave Bill another opportunity to talk about how he 'moves his bones' while acting – something he later curbed: 'When Sam talks about truth and mannerism, I am aware that it has not always been popular what happens to me when I go on stage. I have searched my heart on this and I do think that what I am intending to do is tell a story with all of my body. I am trying to punctuate things, or demonstrate things or indicate whatever might be happening internally in the usual way. I do it perhaps physically to a larger degree than some actors, but I do it instinctively at first. It is partially a result of what happens to me when I am faced with an audience for the first time, which is very, very scary. Opening plays is very scary and the adrenaline is very high, so things occur which you can't anticipate and it's just what happens under that kind of pressure. But then it's up to you, a choice, what you subsequently choose to keep and what you choose to discard. But I have always done it. Now that people refer to it occasionally, it's become more of a choice. As a joke, I used to call it my relentless search for theatrical truth when I appeared with Chiwetel Ejofor and Andrew Lincoln in *Blue/Orange*. They called it me shamelessly trawling for cheap gags. Somewhere between the two, there is the truth.'

But Mendes summed him up more succinctly: 'Suddenly, this sort of weird thing happened. There was this period when suddenly everybody was talking about him, and that was when one became aware of him as a bona fide leading actor in the same bracket as McKellen and Gambon and Dench. He would hesitate, I know, to put himself in that category, but he's absolutely in it.'

Indeed, he took Broadway by storm, receiving the most effusive reviews he has ever enjoyed for a stage role. The *Philadelphia Inquirer* said: 'Bill Nighy is at his twitchiest, and most seductive, slouching across the stage with feline grace, his ironic gaze flirting with us, commenting on every wry or clever remark he makes.'

'Bill Nighy, making his Broadway debut as Hare's worldly Englishman to Julianne Moore's idealistic American, gave one of the most remarkable performances ever seen on a New York stage. A standing ovation is a normal ritual here, as if the audience likes to be seen, too. But when this consummate, cool actor took his bow on the opening night, he was greeted literally by a roar of appreciation and yes, love, that was unique in my Broadway experience.'

Variety.com wrote: 'Rock-star thin and with eyebrows possibly arched since birth, Nighy's rangy physique and in particular his spindly legs are almost as expressive as his softly mocking eyes or droll delivery. His twitchy, loose-limbed body language is so controlled and precise that often he seems to be undermining Moore/Nadia with his feet alone.' UK critics were just as effusive, with the *Guardian* noting: 'It helps that he is played superbly by Bill Nighy, who is a master of tortured idealism. With his seamed features and lean, concave form, Nighy looks like a man who has suffered interestingly. He brings out all the different facets of the faintly twisted Oliver: the flawed father and impenitent seducer, as well as the decent doctor and cool ironist,' while the *Observe*r went even further, saying, 'Nighy gave one of the most remarkable performances ever seen on a New York stage.'

In fact, *New York Times* critic Ben Brantley agreed with many others that Nighy was notably better than both the play and his co-star: 'It is unlikely that any other actor could bring down the house as Mr. Nighy does. Everything he does and every movement he makes is unique.' The *Washington Post* waxed lyrical, saying that every one of Bill's lines in *The Vertical Hour*, 'registers with the effortlessness of one whose wit has been honed over a lifetime of impassioned debate, emboldened by erudition and claret' and that Bill was, 'so natural, one could easily imagine him continuing the performance up the aisles out to the street and into any sociable establishment in town...'

The actor himself was completely unfazed when this particular review was read out to him, commenting:

'Blimey! Has that got any punctuation at all in it? I like the claret mention...'

It is doubtful he would have read any of the reviews, of course, which is sad because he could always do with reassurance that what he does is liked. Opening *The Vertical Hour* was 'beyond tough,' he admitted. 'But then we opened and it was a hit and we sold out, thank God! There is a God. I wasn't quite sure before, but now I know. I got through it and thank the Lord, and it's beautiful because the alternative doesn't bear thinking about.'

Always, he is eternally grateful for a good stage role: 'I grew up in the theatre and I can't see a version of my life where I don't do plays. I have no enthusiasm for that. Even though they put the fear of God into me, I still want to do plays.

'I'm a lucky boy. I've been in world premières of plays which I think will be performed a hundred years from now and this is what I will tell my grandchildren – if they stand still long enough to listen – that I've been spoiled and that most of the best things have been in the theatre. I have worked with Harold Pinter and Tom Stoppard and David Hare and Judi Dench, all of these people, and I've been marvellously lucky that I worked with those writers.'

He has nothing but praise for co-star Dench: 'She has something, which is inexpressible. I guess people have written books about the mystery of how she achieves what she achieves. I did come up with an idea, one way of putting it, is that she does something that very few people are involved in; something very few people attempt. And that is, she arranges to arrive on stage as it were, unarmed, without tricks and without a plan and without some sort of strategy of safety net, which is going to get you out of trouble. She then allows the play to happen to [her]. It requires enormous courage and very few people are at it. She has access to compassionate sensibility, a degree of which not many people seem to have. She is also incredibly funny and a wonderful woman to be around... She's beyond clever. She's very, very, very smart, obviously, and has a great actor's intelligence and is a very clever woman. But there is something beyond that, which is something, an area which not everybody gets to visit.'

His appeal to cinema and theatre audiences alike still baffled him, though. Being called a sex symbol confused him even more: 'I don't really think of it that way. I can't see it lasting for much longer or at least after my jaded disco charm has dried up. I mean, I don't get the girl ever. I don't really get the girl.'

Sir David Hare begged to differ: 'From the moment he walked in the door, I have always thought he was the most interesting actor I have ever seen: incredibly charming and funny in that he wasn't frightened to show his sensitivity and timidity and anxiety. He was a man with a sense of humour about himself. I thought he was the most original, but I couldn't persuade anyone else. There was a self-knowing wit about him, a complexity about a man who knows that a lot of what he does is ridiculous and that seemed terribly modern. This sense that you say something but you can't half help making a joke about it.

'With Bill there is always this slight reluctance to put himself forward. There is a brilliant remark followed by a self-deprecating laugh and it does seem, judging by the reaction of Broadway audiences, that Bill is uniquely attractive to women. I've always thought he was the most remarkably interesting, gifted and brilliant young actor, but I had a great difficulty in the 1980s in persuading the world to my point of view. For many years, I could never get any publicity for him – nobody wanted to talk to Bill. Now the whole world is beating a path to his door. And I think it's the playful, ironic quality that he has that has become so sexual and so profound over the years. The reason that Bill is so modern is that he has a quality we find a lot in life now, where people know that even as they say something, it sounds ridiculous; and that it's both funny and serious at the same time. Bill is original, distinctive, with a very strong personal style of his own, but I don't think the public understood or appreciated that when he was younger. There is something about middle age that has really suited Bill.'

Bill commented: 'That's all very nice, but I wish David had said those things to me 20 years earlier...'

Treading the American stage in such a high-profile project was especially daunting. Bill was known in the States through his screen work, but was an unknown quantity to Broadway theatre audiences. 'I am a new boy here to some extent,' he admitted. And sometimes, his approach to acting – looking and speaking as if events are unfolding for the first time in front of him on stage – was not always understood.

In one of his longest-ever interviews, given on America's *Charlie Rose Show*, he talked about *The Vertical Hour* at length and referred to his realistic technique: 'Someone came and saw the show and we were talking about remembering lines and I said, "It is true that on occasions, actors do forget their lines." He said, "Well, yes, *you* forgot your lines on several occasions, didn't you?" I said, "Well, no I didn't."

'What he had interpreted as me forgetting my lines was something I do to try to make it look more authentic by looking as if I am searching for the words. I sometimes pretend that I can't quite remember the word yet, which is just something people do. It is not rocket science, it is what people do in speech – you know the line but you perhaps try and make it look real. In this case, it backfired on me.'

It is always a shame that he is unsure of his remarkable acting talents – 'An actor the same age as me once came to my trailer and told me we'd probably work forever. I nearly threw him out. I don't want to hear that, I don't take anything for granted.' Sir David Hare sums him up thus: 'Once you have in him in your sights, it's hard to forget him. But also, I think that because he wasn't a "piece of English meat" in his 20s or 30s, he wasn't going to get the parts that Ewan McGregor and those people now get, so he had the opportunity of working on his art. He's now one of the supplest and most interesting film actors, like Helen Mirren, and this degree of expertise is so rare in England. He isn't what you call the traditional macho. He's the man who is witty and good-looking, and looks like you'd have a thoroughly enjoyable evening with before you did what you did, that's what's rare. So many of the young actors are narcissists because all that brooding is about their problems. Bill looks involved in the outside world.'

He returned the compliment, describing Hare as, 'the most influential person on my professional life,' adding, 'and to come to New York in these circumstances and to have it be David's play at this point in my life is, when you feed that into the computer, a pretty good situation for me.' The vulnerability of being on stage, however, still haunts him: 'So much can go wrong, and unlike film work, you don't get a chance at a second take. You are judged by an audience – and critics – on the one performance they see.' And that makes him very uneasy: 'Who needs it, a job where you do this incredibly scary thing? It's unprecedented, it's the première so no one's ever done it before. Over two and a half hours, you have to say all these things, you have to achieve certain things, you have to have a nervous breakdown, make love to somebody, get a few laughs – you know, pour drinks, smoke cigarettes, all this stuff... And then, in the dark, there are all these guys who sit there and they write out a report of what you're doing, and the next day they publish it in a national newspaper. I mean, try it for size. That's a day at work. It's mental; it's odd. Recently I've started having the actor's nightmare, where I walk out on stage and I don't have a costume and don't know my lines. What do you suppose that means?'

In fact, he was sick with fear when *The Vertical Hour* opened, worrying all the time while on stage about how his performance would be received. He was also fighting a cold and it was only into the play's run that he could do the show, 'neither scared nor sick. The sense of relief was inexpressible.' Initially, he found the whole experience horrifying, even though he was hailed in the American press as 'one cool character', a 'middle-aged heart-throb' and 'the one they call when they want an expert...' None of this allayed the anxieties he experienced in the run-up to *The Vertical Hour*'s first performance – or indeed, before he took to the stage for each performance thereafter: 'I love the theatre and I grew up in the theatre and I can't imagine a life not doing plays, even though I retire after every opening night because it is always so scary and so hard, and I always make myself vow that this will never, ever happen to me again.

'It doesn't get any better and nobody tells you that. And when you're young, you assume that opening a play – well, in some way you'll get kind of used to it and it will get easier. It doesn't. It gets worse, I don't know entirely why. Obviously because the expectation is higher, both your own and other people's.

'Other than that I don't really know – and maybe your nervous system gets wired more with age – I don't know, but it's not just me. I know lots of performers, performers I absolutely revere, who've had books written about the mystery of how they achieve what they achieve. And yet I know that they are routinely, you know, nauseous before performances... We all worry, we all say to ourselves, "Christ, what did you do that for, you've put your fucking hand in your fucking pocket – now what are you going to do with the other hand?" You've got to get through the door, take the hand out of the pocket, take the fucking hand out of the fucking pocket, they're all fucking looking at you, and I can't take the hand out of the pocket because they're all fucking looking at me. Of course they're all fucking looking at you – you're on the fucking stage...

'So I am not alone in this. But the opening night in New York was like being – it was one of the greatest nights of my life. But it was also very – the disparity between what was going on in my head during the performance, which was two and a bit of the most unpleasant hours of my life – and then how other people were receiving it, was even by my standards, it was graphically marked. To go on stage to open a play for the first time, for the first few performances, through the press nights and then for the first few performances after that, it is extremely agitating. But then it eases up as you're in the run. Hopefully the thing has gone well and if the show is still good, when everything works, you can go on and just get on with it. But it's the opening which is the tricky part, when there's no precedent for what you have to do, and if you have a healthy paranoia – which I do – it's rich picking for the aliens, for the voice in your head that says, "Are you sure you gonna do this?"

'You know that voice? That voice goes into overdrive and you have to operate whilst listening to the voice. You have to do things despite whatever your head might tell you. For any actor, it's a scary time and a great relief when it's over. The thing is, you imagine when you're younger it's going to get better. And old people are kind enough not to put you straight. Not only does it not get better, I think it probably gets worse. Your expectations of yourself and other people's expectations are greater. The stakes are higher. I thought I was about to be humiliated, you know, internationally speaking, and then they all went mental and started throwing flowers.'

But he need not have had any qualms about how a notoriously hard-to-please Broadway audience would receive him. They loved him. 'Fabulous! Just bloody marvellous,' was how a delighted Bill described those who came to see *The Vertical Hour*. 'They clap when you come on, before you've done anything, which is a phenomenon I've never experienced. I found it a little startling at first, but then I thought, "Well, I could get used to this." They clap when you come on and they stand up at the end, and that's really OK with me. We did two shows one Saturday and got standing ovations at both. You could wait a long time in England for that to happen...'

Once again, his self-doubt was unfounded. He won a Theatre World Award for his portrayal of Oliver Lucas. First presented in 1945, the American award is the oldest granted for a theatre performance, on or off Broadway, and is only given once – as it is presented for a debut. Traditionally, a committee of theatre writers choose six men and six women. On occasion, the awards bestow a Special Theatre World Award on 'performers, casts or others who have made a particularly lasting impression on the New York theatre scene'.

There was an added bonus to his appearance in *The Vertical Hour*: he got to walk on stage to the opening chords of Bob Dylan's *Simple Twist of Fate*. 'I can't believe I walk on to this tune! And that gets me through,' he declared. He also got to meet another of his musical heroes, David Bowie: 'He suddenly materialised in my dressing room. You meet lots of famous people and then there's David Bowie. His achievement is incredible. He was very gracious and charming and it was a big thrill for me.'

The Vertical Hour was a kind of test for him, one that he passed with flying colours: 'The idea of Broadway is something that all English actors have on their list of top five things that might happen to them. That we came here and that it should be successful means a lot to me. I feel I'm legitimate now.'

And so the whole experience of *The Vertical Hour*

was one of the happiest and most rewarding for Bill. He'd been expecting to be cynical about the whole New York thing and wasn't sure about the American culture change. Would he love or hate it? In the end, he discovered he had to agree with New Yorkers that it was a mind-blowing place to spend some time: 'When they said that, I went, "Yeah, yeah," the way you do. Then you come here and it blows your mind! I stand on the street corner and laugh out loud. The policemen look like they're in a movie, the street lights make the city look like a movie set, the trees are all turning and it's fabulous!' Fortunately for the heat-hating Bill, he was in New York at the right time of year to enjoy his beloved autumnal weather. Summer in the city would not have suited him at all.

The Vertical Hour finished its run on 3 November 2007. He admitted this was one of the best times of his life: 'I've had some times, but professionally, yes, this is easily one of the best. Things have happened to me that I had no way of expecting or that I hadn't anticipated and the period in New York doing David's play with Julianne Moore, one of the actresses I most admire in the world, who's been so fabulous, directed by Sam Mendes, one of the greatest directors currently operating, and then to see Stephen Poliakoff's film *Gideon's Daughter* honoured in America and to see young Emily Blunt win a prize also. To be in one piece and enjoying this kind of work is very important.'

Bill singled out Julianne Moore for special praise, saying, 'the air changes when she goes to work, she is one of those people. There are lots of very, very good actors around and then there is a shorter list that contains names like Julianne and Dame Judi Dench. Julianne and I did the play for some time, eight times a week, and there was never, ever, one moment when we did not aim for the stars every night. She works at a very, very high level and you hardly have to think. Everything just becomes a natural response to what she's doing. It's beautiful.' She, in turn, returned the compliment, saying, 'No one is able to get a joke the way Bill can get a joke.'

Chapter Nine

Storming the Box Office

Bill is, of course, acutely aware that for him, fame and recognition came later in life than most. However, he finds it amusing that he is thought to have suddenly appeared from nowhere, when, just like all other working actors, he had quietly been getting on with the job in hand for years.

'I don't have a problem with it, I am just very grateful,' he admits. 'It is true that I enjoy now a degree of attention that I didn't get before, but it's also true that I've had a great career in my terms. I've always been lucky; I've always worked with people who I admire – great men and women I've worked with over the years. In the theatre, I've had as good a career as you could possibly have. I have done world premières of great plays by great writers and I have worked with great actors. I have always had a gig and it was always a good one. And the fact that people didn't get to hear about it in such large numbers is not a problem to me.

But there are occasionally times when it is as if I have been idling, as if I have been hanging around the house, and suddenly I get good. I am the only person with all the information. You just have to keep your manners and keep your sense of humour. The fact is, I have been working it on a while and I am just very happy. I have got better over the years. I am desperately temperamentally unsuited for the job…'

During the year he added his vocals to another animation, this time *Flushed Away*, written by his former workmates, Dick Clement and Ian La Frenais as well as Sam Fell and Peter Lord. (A host of other writers, including Simon Nye, contributed to the screenplay.) Bill played Whitey, a rat henchman to Ian McKellen's Toad overlord. Andy Serkis played Spike, the other henchman, sent to track down and catch cute rats, Rita and Roddy (Kate Winslet and Hugh Jackman). He found the experience interesting, albeit a little weird: 'It's kind of strange actually, at first, but it's a free process. You're able to do things over and over and over again, so you can hone it down. I was playing an albino, ex-lab rat with brain damage from over-exposure to hallucinogens and he's therefore not the brightest spark in the pack. And I get to sing various songs. The last time I was there, I did a duet [with Kate Winslet] on *Close to You* by the Carpenters. And they let me sing the whole song. I do sometimes love my job – you walk into the booth and you're a brain-damaged rat and they want you to sing a Carpenters song! That's when I start to get interested – it's a cool way to make a living.'

The film garnered praise not only in the UK but worldwide too, with US reviewer James Berardinelli calling it a 'breath of fresh air' and hailing the voice castings as 'genius.'

That same year, Bill appeared briefly in the £25m epic *Stormbreaker*, playing the MI6 boss Alan Blunt, who recruits young Alex Rider. Directed by Geoffrey Sax and based on the novel by Anthony Horowitz, Mickey Rourke, Ewan McGregor, Damian Lewis, Alicia Silverstone and Sophie Okonedo also starred. It was shot on location on the Isle of Man – described by Bill as a cross 'between Cornwall and Ireland'. For him, it was a happy return to the island as he has filmed there many times.

The Isle of Man's ability to become any country, from England to France or Germany, makes it a highly popular choice with filmmakers. *Stormbreaker*'s author Anthony Horowitz describes it as a 'chameleon of an island' and Bill is fond of the place because it allows British films under a certain budget to be made. 'I like the island very much. I've been there lots of times on many different films and thank God for the Isle of Man!' he declared.

He was back on the island again in July of that year with Anthony Horowitz and producer Marc Samuelson at a black-tie gala presentation of *Stormbreaker* at the Villa Marina. The VIP guests were more than happy to mingle with fans at the champagne reception, a charity event aimed at raising money for the Isle of Man's Children's Centre. Bill commented: 'I will use any excuse to come to the island – the people are very pleasant and happy to see us, and I'm very proud of the film. I have had a very long and very satisfying association with the Isle of Man. Just as a place, I am always happy here. The work I have done in the Isle of Man, I am as proud of as anything in my career.'

Within days of opening, on 13 October 2006, *Stormbreaker* smashed through the £1m mark at the box office. It was one simple scene, with Bill loudly munching on a biscuit before the lead-in to boots marching in a training camp, which delighted critics and audiences alike. Said director Geoffrey Sax: 'It was literally a last-minute idea on the set. I asked the prop man if he had any biscuits and of course you give Bill a comedy moment and he gives you so much more than you expect.'

Worldwide, Bill won rave reviews for his role of Blunt. The *Sydney Morning Herald* wrote: 'The biggest bonus is the appearance of Bill Nighy as MI6 spymaster Mr Blunt. He's Alex's recruiter – his M, if you like – and he's blunt by name and nature. With a battleship-grey complexion and a wardrobe of suits to match, he has a mirthless snort of a laugh, a gimlet-eyed gaze and a robotic array of tics and twitches that keep him in motion.' Closer to home, *The Times* commented: 'Bill Nighy is a camp and deadpan joy as the careless boss of the Secret Service, Mr Blunt. He wears Eric Morecambe glasses and a thin moustache, and every line he utters is a clipped and sardonic masterpiece.'

Perhaps one of the biggest accolades came from the American newspaper, *Seattle Weekly*, whose critic stated that Bill delivered, 'more entertainment value with one eyebrow than everyone else in the movie combined.' And while he won critical acclaim, he also won the affections of one of his young co-stars, Alicia Silverstone, who was later to declare of the 56-year-old actor: 'I developed a bit of a crush on Bill. In fact, I really loved him...' A couple of years earlier, actress Emilia Fox had described him as 'the sexiest man on screen.'

Professionally, his life was very much on the up. It seemed success had been a long time coming and now Bill wanted to grab it with both hands. He had become an almost obsessive workaholic, once admitting, 'All actors who have been around for a long time – which I have – and have been skint for long periods – which I have – find it difficult to turn down jobs. If I turn anything down, my stomach turns over; I feel sick. It feels like gambling.'

In between work commitments, just as when he was a young man, he preferred to be alone, listening to Bob Dylan and drinking strong Yorkshire tea. But for him, the solitude he liked to engineer for himself was now often forced upon him by the separations caused by being one half of an acting couple. 'Eating alone in Thai restaurants is a large part of my life, because my wife is an actress and therefore we're always apart,' he remarked.

Once more, he was facing his own demons. Now, he

saw work as his saviour. In 2007, he teamed up again with his old friend Simon Pegg in *Hot Fuzz*, a police spoof directed by Edgar Wright, in which Pegg plays a hot shot detective, who embarrasses his bosses by being too good at his job and is therefore shipped off to a quiet country backwater. Bill plays the Met Chief Inspector, who does the dirty on him, backed by officious Inspector Frank Butterman (Jim Broadbent).

Said Bill: 'I did it because I love them and because they sweet-talked me. But Simon Pegg and Edgar Wright, who are the star and director respectively – and who also co-wrote the script of *Shaun of the Dead* – are wonderful guys. They can write really funny jokes and they got everybody in this movie. It's a big, daft, stupid cop movie. It's basically city cop goes rural and Simon again plays the hero with Nick [Frost] as his sidekick. I'm the most important cop there is. I shouldn't tell you this, not that it matters terribly much, but I'm a very important policeman. It's my first time playing a policeman and I'm very proud to be the most important one in the whole picture.'

Hot Fuzz also starred Martin Freeman, Edward Woodward, Stephen Merchant, David Threlfall, Steve Coogan (in an uncredited cameo) and Billie Whitelaw. Bill's acting friend and almost regular co-star, Cate Blanchett, played Jeanine (again, uncredited). Edgar Wright was nominated for Best Director in the 2008 *Empire* Awards. Pegg was actually nominated for the 2008 *Empire* Award for Best Actor. More fittingly, he won the UK National Movie Awards of 2007 for Best Comedy.

Hot Fuzz was released on 14 February 2007 and grossed around $50m worldwide. It also spawned a huge following, in the US and the UK, who urged each other on via the *Hot Fuzz* website to enter into the spirit of things by doing everything from 'Support your favourite character from *Hot Fuzz* by doing your best impersonation and dressing up' (America) to 'We need your help to create a dictionary of British slang used in *Hot Fuzz*' (Britain). Bill is always grateful for his British following: 'I do quite nicely in Britain. You can be a working actor here.'

Then the film he had worked 'back-to-back' on towards the end of 2005 and early 2006 was finally released in 2007. *Pirates of the Caribbean: At World's End* saw him (or rather *didn't* see him) again playing the computer generated Davy Jones. But the old team was back in force – Orlando Bloom as Will Turner, Geoffrey Rush (Barbossa), Johnny Depp as Jack Sparrow, while Keira Knightley played Elizabeth Swann. Rolling Stone Keith Richards had a cameo as Jack Sparrow's dad, a challenge that apparently left him 'tried and emotional' during one day's filming.

This time, the plot had the crew of the *Black Pearl* rescuing Jack Sparrow (Depp) from Davy Jones' Locker and then preparing to fight the East India Trading Company, led by Cutler Beckett (Tom Hollander) and Davy Jones. Our heroes and heroines call on the Pirate Lords from around the world. The Pirate Lords want to release the goddess Calypso, Davy Jones' damned lover (yes, apparently even half-squid, half-crab monsters can have a love interest) from the trap they sent her to, in the hope that she will help them fight.

The Disney film, again directed by Gore Verbinski, was released on 24 May 2007. Critical reviews were mixed, with many stating the plot was too convoluted. The *Scotsman* wrote: 'The story is too complicated to follow or even to explain. Roughly speaking, it is a race to capture the heart of Davy Jones, which lies beating on its own in a small wooden chest. Jones, understandably enough, would quite like to be reunited with his vital organ, as its absence has played havoc with his complexion, though it is reassuring to note that even beneath a nest of computerised squid tendrils, Bill Nighy's funny twitch remains visible.'

But audiences loved the film, causing reviewer Alex Billington to remark: 'This is just how the film industry works nowadays; critics give bad opinions, the public usually has a differing opinion, and all is well in the world of Hollywood since the studios made their millions, anyway.'

At World's End was the most successful movie that year, grossing around $960m worldwide (making it the second most popular of the *Pirates*' trilogy behind *Dead Man's Chest*). It could also claim to be the most expensive film ever produced, at a cost of nearly $300m. *At World's End* was nominated for two Academy Awards – Makeup and Special Effects. In addition, it was voted Best Movie and Best 'Threequel' at the People's Choice Awards, with

Johnny Depp and Keira Knightley both winning awards for their performances.

But Bill was not to secure the Best Supporting Actor award that director Gore Verbinski was convinced would come his way. Before the film was released, the director even told the cast and crew to get his acceptance speech ready. But it was not to be. If there was any disappointment, then Bill did not show it, saying: 'I don't mind – I am in one of the biggest-grossing movies the world has ever seen. And it was a lot of hard work, and I'm in it, albeit in a strange form. I don't mind. I'll settle for that, that's fine.' And he had nothing but praise for award-winning Depp, saying: 'Johnny's a brilliant man, and a wonderful man, as well and exemplary co-worker. When I first arrived, we worked out a few scenes together – there were some small accidents and he's extremely inventive, he never stops working. He's fabulous to work with.'

Above all, in *At World's End* good conquered evil, much to the satisfaction of cinema fans. Verbinski remarked: 'I felt it important that the third film was the end of an era – like in a postmodern Western, where the railroad comes and the gunfighter is extinct. It seemed that we had an opportunity to take a look at a world where the legitimate has become corrupt and there is no place for honest thieves in that society, so you have darker issues and a little melancholy. The myths are dying. That seemed a great theme with which to complete the trilogy.'

Ultimately, Bill did receive an award of sorts for the

film. It was the Teen Choice Sleazebag Award, which could be considered some accolade for his thoroughly unpleasant Davy Jones. His New York appearance in *The Vertical Hour* meant that he was unable to be present to accept the award in person, but he said that had he been able to do so, then he would have been most gracious in his acceptance speech: 'I was honoured by it. And if I could have thought of something to say, I would have given a big "up" to all sleazebags and I would have declared myself their new leader, very proudly.'

It had certainly been a filming challenge for him and the rest of the crew on the back-to-back shooting of *Dead Man's Chest* and *At World's End*. *Dead Man's Chest* finished on 1 March 2006 and filming resumed in August of that year at the Bonneville Salt Flats, Utah (for Davy Jones' Locker scenes), continuing off the coast of California. The climactic battle was shot in a former air hanger at Palmdale, California, where the cast had to wear wetsuits beneath their costumes. Eventually, filming finished on 10 January 2007, with a world première on 19 May of that year.

But it wasn't just a heavy professional workload that Bill was taking on. In June, the avid reader got involved with Silksoundbooks, a website offering new readings of classic literature, which could be downloaded onto iPods and MP3 players. Bill joined an illustrious crew, including Judi Dench, Jane Horrocks, Lindsay Duncan, Edward Fox, Richard E. Grant and Greta Scacchi. All waived half or all their performance fees in favour of taking shares in Silksoundbooks.

Bill was the very first actor to join the project and his contributions to the readings were his favourite book, *Parade's End* by Ford Maddox Ford and Edgar Allan Poe's *The Dupin Mysteries* (which he spent a whole day recording while in New York and of which *Guardian* journalist Sue Arnold commented: 'Whoever chose to combine Poe's ghoulishly gory and violent script with Nighy's famously low-key, deadpan delivery knew what they were doing – it's a powerful brew'. Bill told David Smith of the *Observer*: 'I love books and the idea of reading them out loud. I passionately support the idea of recording great books at a very cheap price. The idea that you can download a major novel and have it read to you in the car is sweet. It introduces literature in an entertaining way and the idea that these wonderful books are being spread across the world thrills me.

'It's quite hard reading a book, as you have to do all the voices. I have been told I do women quite well. I read *War and Peace* once – I only had two days to get the hang of all those names. I also read one where the narrator was a Native American, who went to North Korea, then Siberia, with lots of Russian tribes, then Japan – I thought, "God almighty, why me?"' But he was enthusiastic about a project, which involved actors in such a comfortable way: 'There is an actors' company atmosphere and I like the idea of being a shareholder – I've never had shares in anything before.'

Of course, anything involving books would have an almost magnetic allure: 'The thrill of walking into a well-appointed bookshop is one of my favourite things.' Like any passionate reader, Bill has his firm favourites. In an interview with *Easy Living* magazine, he listed his top six:

Parade's End by Ford Maddox Ford: '*Parade's End* is probably my favourite book of all time. I discovered it about ten years ago and I'm with W.H. Auden, who said, "There are not many English novels which deserve to be called great: *Parade's End* is one of them."'

The First Forty-Nine Stories by Ernest Hemingway: 'I read this when I was a teenager and it altered the course of my life – Hemingway's stories were so powerful, they just drove me nuts. I left home on the strength of them and the first Bob Dylan album.'

A Dance to the Music of Time by Anthony Powell: 'It took me a year to read all 12 volumes. I was away filming a great deal, and it became the day's highlight. When I stopped being a vampire or a faded, middle-aged rock star, I was allowed to go to bed and take *A Dance to the Music of Time* with me and have a cup of tea.'

Amongst Women by John McGahern: '*Amongst Women* is one of the greatest books I've read. It's such a wonderful book that when I learn that someone hasn't read it, I always tell them to do so immediately.'

Collected Poems & Prose by Harold Pinter: 'Pinter's *I Know The Place* is my favourite poem. It's so beautiful – I'd like it to be my epitaph. I'm a romantic, but I don't feel any shame – I just sigh because it's quite hard work.'

As mentioned earlier, his other favourite work is the play *Skylight* by his close friend, Sir David Hare.

In June 2007, Bill took more time out from stage and screen to help launch an appeal to save the Bristol Old Vic theatre, which closed in August of that year for an 18-month refurbishment. Around £2m was needed to save the theatre and he joined actors, including Tim Piggott-Smith, Judi Dench, Timothy West, Donald Sinden and Simon Callow, to safeguard the future of the illustrious building, which he described as 'this famously distinguished theatre, which should be on the National Health.'

Another nice little project came in October when he was invited to read *Eric Clapton: The Autobiography* on BBC Radio 2. That same year, he made a guest appearance in *Coping Strategies*, a 26-minute black comedy film about Shahid, a young man with learning disabilities, who wants to break free of his mother and find romance. Bill played Julian, a social worker.

The play was produced by Yarrow Housing Organisation's Moment by Moment Theatre Group, with whom Bill worked after hearing of the organisation's aims to improve the quality of life for those with learning problems, to help them be independent in their own homes. In an interview with the *Guardian*, he said: 'Yarrow has become dear to my heart because I think there is a lot of misunderstanding about the ability of people with learning difficulties to integrate successfully into society. There is no reason why the majority of them cannot lead normal lives, live in normal dwellings and have normal employment and normal relationships, and that is what Yarrow is all about.'

He was full of praise for the theatre group, saying: 'Because everyone is on an equal footing in the Moment by Moment Theatre Company, they stop seeing themselves as a person with, or without a disability. They simply become just actors working together.'

That was exactly what *Coping Strategies* director Adam Koronka wanted to achieve. He said, 'We concentrate on what the cast can do – and challenge them to do that well – in order to overcome some of the things they may find more difficult. Our aim is for audiences to enjoy the experience because it is funny, exciting, poignant and tight, rather than just worthy... With that in mind, *Coping Strategies* was created. The cast is drawn from talent we developed through our last four productions – with the welcome addition of the well-known actor Bill, who plays a zealously "right-on" social worker. Filming has been a very different experience to rehearsing and performing a live show. The advantage of a film is, though, that the end-product will hopefully be enjoyed and understood by a much wider audience than a stage show could reach – and in so doing be a catalyst for many more dreams to fly and many more barriers to fall.'

Although just a minor project for Bill in his now heavy workload – he fitted it in between filming the thriller *Valkyrie* about a wartime plot to assassinate Hitler – it was deeply satisfying. He said of the theatre group: 'They are such terrific fun, and they do such valuable and entertaining work... Some of the actors have difficulty communicating in the beginning, and all of that disappears.'

Though he might have found his involvement in *Coping Strategies* satisfying, he did not attend the première screening at the Riverside Studios in Hammersmith, on 16 October 2007. This might have been because he was busy with his involvement in a BBC Radio 4 play to be broadcast at the end of that month, in which he played the actor and amateur sleuth Charles Paris in *Murder Unprompted.* As the seedy, middle-aged actor (you can see *why* Bill felt he was perfect for the part!), Charles is his own worst enemy – a lush who can resist anything but temptation, especially in the form of women and alcohol. His intentions may be good, but somehow it always goes wrong. Charles finally has a shot at the big time. Cast as a second billing in a new play that is going down well in fringe theatre, he looks as though he might make it to the West End. His hopes are cruelly dashed when the play's investors insist on 'big names' in their production – one of them is shot dead on stage on the opening night.

A few months later, he was back as Charles Paris in *Sicken and So Die*, broadcast on 3 March 2008, on BBC Radio 4 – 'Tune in and enjoy a role that seems to have been written for him' – extolled his fan site billnighy.com. Three other Charles Paris stories were broadcast over the next three weeks.

A glimpse into his hectic workload was given in a letter he took time out to write for one of his fan websites that April. It makes interesting reading, with Bill referring to his filming schedules crammed into 2008 – and the music he was listening to at the time of penning the note.

He hadn't forgotten his other concerns, though. For Bill, charity is as big an element in life as acting. In February he sketched a minimalist picture of a house, cliff, sea – and planet in the sky – for National Doodle Day. He was joining other celebrities to help raise funds for The Neurofibromatosis Association and Epilepsy Action (NSE), of which he is an ambassador. At the end of 2004, he launched a partnership between NSE and EasyJet, whose big-hearted passengers went on to donate £200,000. All the celebrity doodles were auctioned on eBay on 7 March. Bill feels that publicising NSE and raising funds is vital for an often-misunderstood condition: 'NSE is at the cutting edge of research into the causes and treatment of epilepsy working towards a goal of seizure freedom for all.'

He was back doodling in September when he donated a picture that looked like three swans with three seagulls in the background! Strangely, again a mysterious ringed planet featured. Bill's caption was a slightly enigmatic, too: 'Snow snored, like a big dog, all over town'. This time, his artistic efforts were for the charity auction 'Pushing the Envelope', designed to raise funds for the National Literacy Trust. Once again, his work was among a 'celebrity lot' auctioned on eBay in October.

In November, dog-loving Bill took part in a radio advertisement to support the RSPCA's Firework Campaign. It was broadcast between 1 and 5 November and featured David Schneider trying to put earplugs into his cat's ears to protect it from firework noise. Bill tells him that using earplugs on animals is 'stupid' and instead asks listeners to text 'BANG' to the RSPCA at 60022 for better advice on how to help animals.

Bill remarked: 'I'm delighted to support the RSPCA's fireworks campaign and I hope the ad will help remind people that fireworks frighten thousands of pets. This is a huge problem, and I hope everyone will do what they can to help. The best thing people can do is go to an organised public display instead of holding their own at home – and encourage the organisers to use lower noise fireworks.'

His big film project of 2008 was the aforementioned *Valkyrie*, starring opposite Tom Cruise and working with Tom Wilkinson, Kenneth Branagh and Eddie Izzard, among others. The film eventually opened in the UK, in February 2009, after the release dates were changed four times. In interviews before *Valkyrie* hit the cinemas, Bill refuted suggestions there had been behind-the-scenes worries, insisting completion was delayed to shoot extra scenes. He told MTV: 'They've added some new stuff, and people are very excited about it.'

The new scenes were 'big-budget' action ones set in North Africa to show how Cruise's character Colonel

Claus von Stauffenberg – based on a real-life soldier who headed a plot to assassinate Hitler – lost an eye. Bill played General Friedrich Olbricht, a military hero charged with the responsibility of setting Operation Valkyrie in motion. His character was largely sympathetic, though his hesitation in carrying out his anti-Hitler duties provided a major plot (and historical) element.

He did not attempt a German accent, but nor did Cruise – 'The story carries the audience along,' explained Bill. 'Hopefully, the actors embody the characters they're playing well enough that most audience members aren't constantly aware of accents and such. After all, this is not a documentary. It is a sort of adventure film, certainly a suspense film.'

He praised what he saw as Cruise's bravery in taking the part. 'It required courage, because the world would be watching and waiting. Whenever something is historically inspired, there is going to be more of a spotlight and more room for criticism.' He also found his fellow actor's enthusiasm rubbed off on him: 'He works harder than anybody I've ever come across. I am a negative English man who likes to slack off and my whole agenda is, "When do I get to sit down?" It is inspirational, seriously, to be around such positivity because I don't manufacture it on my own time!'

The role appealed to him for a number of reasons: because Bryan Singer was directing, Tom Cruise would be starring with him, and he has some fascination for World War Two. Plus, as he said, 'It's a great story.' He told Hollywood film critic, Paul Fischer: 'I'm interested in that period. I don't know, really, why, but maybe it's an English thing, or a European thing. I can't have nostalgia for it obviously, because I wasn't quite around at that time, but everybody I know of my generation is kind of fascinated by it. I did read once that everyone has a kind of nostalgia for the period 60 years before they were born. I mean, before now, kind of thing. It's a sort of perennial thing. Everyone has a kind of generalized nostalgia for a period of that length of time before. But, I don't know... Obviously it's a very evocative time and it was – you know, the stories are very big there. It was a time when our country, England, was briefly unified and that people were democratized by being in great peril. So, it was a very interesting time, socially and culturally.'

He also revealed to Fischer that he had to work at creating the character of Olbricht: 'I suppose you could say it's how it occurred to me. It's not in the script, particularly, except that it's made plain in the script, that the way he's presented, as much as he's presented in the script, is that he was a hesitant, diffident, cautious man. So I suppose that the idea of that somehow would, to some degree, have informed my decision to kind of keep it low-key. And I thought that might work and get people's attention in the midst of all the hullaballoo.'

In another interview about the role, he admitted that he had great admiration for Olbricht: 'I never thought of him as a Nazi. In spirit he wasn't. He had to pay lip service to the Nazi Party to stay alive... These men were in the midst of a country terrified into collective madness. They were honourable military men, ashamed that they had a commander-in-chief who was not only an incompetent corporal, but also a lunatic. Olbricht was involved in the German resistance longer than almost anyone else. He risked his life every day for several years, plotting schemes against Hitler. And then, when the moment of real action arrived, he faltered. The two officers were to die for their beliefs.'

Bryan Singer chose Bill for the part of Olbricht because of his 'likeability' needed to counterbalance Olbricht's character. In turn, Bill praised the director's 'wonderful job of re-creating atmosphere as well as incredible suspense. What makes it all the more incredible is the fact that we know how it turns out. We know that all the assassination plots against Hitler failed, that he survived until the end of the war, and only then took his own life. He waited until he had all but destroyed Germany before abdicating his insane and evil dream, or nightmare. Yet even knowing the outcome, this film is almost unrelentingly suspenseful.'

One of the eeriest and most moving experiences for him during the making of *Valkyrie* was filming on the exact spot in Berlin where Olbricht faced a firing squad: 'Bryan and Tom made a little speech that night just to mark the occasion, out of respect and to recognise that we were being given this responsibility to show how these brave men lived and died.' He was also quite shaken by actor David Bamber's portrayal of

Hitler: 'He was too eerily like him. He looked very, very spookily like the man. As an actor, you're used to seeing all kinds of people dressed up as all kinds of things, and it becomes routine to see people in ridiculous things or funny things, or outlandish things or space sci-fi things, or whatever – I've played a squid, for crying out loud – but there's nothing that prepares you when somebody walks in and looks exactly like Adolf Hitler.'

Generally, Bill gets on well with all his co-stars and Tom Cruise was no exception. The two got along famously, despite their cultural – and height – differences. Bill remarked: 'He's a very easy, satisfying guy to work with. And we all got along pretty well, and we slipped into a nice ensemble feeling. There was never any hint that he was – you know, head of the studio, or any of that kind of status crap. He was a democrat about things. I never felt that and I don't think anybody else did.'

Although he played a German way back in 1985 in the TV film *Hitler's SS: Portrait in Evil*, Bill did not feel comfortable wearing a Nazi uniform, describing it as 'one of the most disconcerting things imaginable... It's so associated with evil that it took me several days to get used to being in costume.'

Valkyrie was released in the USA on Christmas Day 2008 and took over £20m in its first weekend. Bill admitted the character of Olbricht was one of the 'most riveting' he had ever played: 'An actor's work is often illuminating to himself, though often it just illuminates something about himself. In this case, going to Germany and before that, learning so much about the assassination plot, I learned a lot. Not just about history, which is of course important, because we know that all too often it can repeat itself, but about human beings: what they are capable of, how they react and why. But then, on top of this huge dollop of knowledge and experience that I, as an actor was granted, to be able to share this with audiences around the world. It's... well, it is awesome.'

Chapter Ten

Groovy Old Man on a Serious Mission

Though Bill was still experiencing difficulties in coming to terms with the fact that he was wanted as an actor, that now he was the first choice of writers and directors, he tried to take it all in his lanky stride, balancing the feeling of accomplishment with the concern that one day, it might just evaporate. He told Ariel Leve of the *Sunday Times*: 'Nothing much has changed. There's not a lot to handle. The work has changed – and that's good. What's happened is, it's made me much more useful and castable and I have choices now that I'm very, very grateful for. And it's astonishing, this late in the game. But I wasn't waiting for it to happen; it's an uncertain life and nobody's progress is assured. Like every English actor, the major concern if you have a family is to get through the month – get through the year. I've always been lucky, I've always had a gig.'

In between big-screen appearances, his profile was maintained elsewhere too. In April 2008, he was heard on M Radio in *Strangers on a Train* by Patricia Highsmith, adapted from the classic Hitchcock film of 1951. Originally broadcast on 25 January 1996, on BBC Radio 4's Cinema 100 season, the play was directed by Andy Jordan. Any Hitchcock fans will know the plot well. Architect Guy Haines wants to divorce his unfaithful wife Miriam so that he can marry the woman he truly loves – US senator's daughter Anne Morton. While on a train travelling to see his wife, he meets Charles Anthony Bruno, who talks about how he would like to see his father out of his life. Bruno comes up with the idea of the two men 'exchanging murders', with him offering to kill Miriam, if Haines will kill his father in return.

On 1 May 2008, BBC Radio 7 had three repeats of Bill's radio play, *Killing Maestros*, first aired in 2003. Directed by Liz Webb, he played conductor Sergei Bodanov, who is convinced he will be the next to die. He joined a cast which included Henry Goodman, Lorelei King and Sylvestra La Touzel. The play was previewed as 'a must-hear for Bill Nighy fans'. Two days later, you could hear him on the radio again in *Cigarettes and Chocolate*, a Radio 4 tribute to writer and director Anthony Minghella, who had recently died. The Giles Cooper Award-winning production had Bill playing alongside Juliet Stevenson and told the story of a woman called Gemma, her unexplained silence, refusal to speak and how her circle of friends and lovers react. It was first broadcast some 20 years before.

In June of that year, BBC 7 repeated Bill's reading of George Orwell's *Animal Farm*. Three months later, he was to be heard on BBC 7, on 26 August, with three broadcasts of *Vongole*, in which he played Professor Swann, who seduced his students over plates of spaghetti vongole. The play was to have two more airings, both on 28 March 2009.

Also that year, Bill appeared in the short film *Slapper*. This was the directing debut of acclaimed actor Chiwetel Ejofor, who had played Peter, the husband of Juliet, Keira Knightley's character, in *Love Actually*.

Slapper was screened on 24 June 2008 as part of the UK shorts programme at the Edinburgh Film Festival. The cast comprised Kieran Bew, Nathaniel Gleed, Iain Glen, Lloyd Hutchinson, Melanie Kilburn, Cal Macaninch, Keith Martin, Anthony Rosato, Peter Wight and Benedict Wong. Bill played a character called Arnold Percy in the 22-minute short, which was about a boy missing his father and a man struggling to provide for his family. All is settled in the final round of a competitive slapping tournament between national hero Jack Sinclair and the mysterious challenger 'Red'.

In the second week of July, Bill took time out from acting to focus on social and moral responsibilities. He attended the G8 summit in Tokyo on behalf of Oxfam to lobby about the lack of world aid. The *Observer* was fortunate to secure his diary for the visit. It made fascinating reading and gave an amazing insight into a man who, while passionate about acting, recognises there are greater issues that he needs to put his mind to. It was his second time in Tokyo – he had filmed *Pirates of the Caribbean* there.

Despite suffering jetlag and lack of sleep, he patiently became the subject of many photo sessions and interviews and attended several gatherings throughout the visit to publicise his cause, including one at the British Embassy as a guest of the ambassador, Sir Graham Fry. There, he listened to British Prime Minister's wife, Sarah Brown, and the Japanese Prime Minister's wife, Kiyoko Fukuda, speaking on behalf of the White Ribbon Alliance, which he described as, '...the admirable and fast-growing organisation concerned with safe motherhood. The women spoke eloquently and powerfully about the terrible situation of women dying in childbirth in developing countries. It's the one UN Millennium Development Goal around which there has been zero movement. Currently, 500,000 women die completely unnecessarily every year in childbirth, which in turn creates at least a million orphans every year. Having heard Sarah Brown speak before, I was not surprised that she was inspiring and clever.'

There was also a two-hour drive to Sapporo, 'where the alternative G8 summit takes place', to be grilled by journalists. Almost inevitably, there was the suggestion that Bill was simply a celebrity jumping on a charitable bandwagon of such crucial importance to ease his own conscience: 'A reporter asked me how I would respond to "people" who said I was just a celebrity trying to feel good about himself. I should have asked for the names of those "people", but couldn't think quickly enough. I also probably should have answered that two children die every minute from malaria, 5,000 children die every day from dirty water and 30,000 children die from other causes occasioned by extreme poverty every 24 hours. This is entirely and easily preventable, but again I couldn't think quickly enough.

'What I, in fact, said was that I would tell these "people", if it was any comfort to them, that I don't feel good about myself. I have a long history of not feeling good about myself... I have not suddenly become an expert on international affairs. Nor have I developed greater access to my compassionate sensibility than anyone else. I have simply been alerted to certain facts and I have been assured by people who dedicate their lives to the subject that extreme poverty cannot only be eradicated, it can be easily eradicated. Recently, the rich countries raised a trillion dollars to bail out the banks. They did it in six months so it can be done. The poor need a fraction of that money.

In British terms, it's about 60p per person per year. It's a tenth of the money that was required to invade Iraq. Currently, 880 million people are undernourished and dying from things that we stopped dying from 100 years ago. They're not asking for money – we are. Intelligent aid in all forms, including long-term budget support over a number of years, would make those countries self-supporting and finally balance the planet. We wouldn't even notice. One day, we'd look round and Africa would be shining and nobody would have to listen to me banging on.'

In between the business to hand, he did manage to get in some leisure time: to his great embarrassment being caught out yet again playing air guitar – 'I vowed this time I wouldn't do it!' – eating sushi (he is a late convert to the Japanese speciality) and shopping: 'I like the supermarkets in Tokyo. They remind me of shops when I was a child and there's something about the packaging and the designs here that I find appealing. Last time I was in Tokyo, I bought 16 napkins designed by Vivienne Westwood and the trip to the wrapping station in the store was as exciting as the purchase. You were given a choice of paper then shown the wrapper ribbon chart, whereupon the lady performed a lightning act of origami worthy of Rowan Atkinson in *Love Actually*. She then bowed several times as she gave them to me. I could get used to this.'

He also penned a blog about his visit, re-enforcing his commitment as genuinely caring rather than just getting on the charitable bandwagon: 'Working with Oxfam, I haven't become an expert on international affairs, but I have done a couple of films about developing countries. One was *The Constant Gardener*, which was about the great modern scandal of how Africa is used as a laboratory for testing new medicines. I also acted in *The Girl in the Café*, directed by Richard Curtis, playing a civil servant at a G8 forum in Iceland, so that's probably why I was an obvious choice for Oxfam to ask me to be their ambassador. The film was quite similar to the real thing; they did a good job of getting the overall tone, creating a mixture of excitement and dread at the same time.

'My message to the G8 leaders is, and will remain: "Keep your promises". If they don't, the world will be facing a critical situation in which millions of lives will be lost, even though the solution is achievable, easily achievable. The people of Oxfam know that better than anyone.'

He also put his name to a letter, signed by other concerned parties, about climate change and the world's poor which was published in *The Times* on 9 December that year:

Sir,
In the face of economic crisis we have seen what is achievable when countries unite in a common cause. But with the world at the brink of ecological disaster and millions of poor people already living on the front line of climate change, it is essential that this ambition be heightened as world leaders meet this week at the UN climate negotiations in Poland.

Around the world, international aid agencies such as Oxfam are seeing the effects of climate change on the world's poor. In Uganda, changing weather patterns mean farmers gamble when to sow seeds; in Bangladesh, more intense and frequent monsoons have destroyed homes.

Around the world, health is at risk from disease and malnutrition, and children – usually girls – are being pulled from school to walk further distances for water. It is desperately unfair that the poor should again feel the brunt, despite being least responsible. Wealthy nations, who are in their advantaged position because of heavy industrialisation, are the most responsible and most able to lead the world in tackling climate change. This is why they must show leadership in Poland and provide solutions that have the interests of the world's poor at their heart.

Rich countries must lead the way to cut emissions now so that all countries take their fair share of responsibility and act to keep global warming from? exceeding 2°C above pre-industrial levels. They must also commit funding so that poor communities can adapt to climate change. Together, we must work towards low-carbon development so that all countries – including the poor – can prosper.

We call on world leaders meeting in Poznan to ensure that these ingredients are put in place. Only then can we hope for a global climate agreement that will safeguard the planet and ensure that poor people can truly pull themselves from poverty.

Archbishop Emeritus Desmond Tutu, Sheila Watt-Cloutier, Janina Ochojska, Gael García Bernal, Ian McEwan, Sir David Attenborough, Kristin Davis,

Rahul Bose, Jarvis Cocker, Colin Firth, Annie Lennox, Angelique Kidjo, Iain Banks, Scarlett Johansson, Bill Nighy, Thom Yorke, Missy Higgins, Mark Lynas, Miguel Bosé

It was not the first time that Bill had highlighted the work of Oxfam. In 2007, he became an ambassador for the charity and that June, frustrated by the slow progress of G8 leaders delivering aid to poor countries following the G8 summit two years earlier, he travelled to Tanzania to visit schools. He was shocked to see classes of 100 pupils, a huge increase since primary education there became free in 2001; he also visited hospitals, women's groups and food and water projects in the remote Ngorongoro District. Commenting on his visit, he said that it had given him hope that, 'if rich countries keep their aid promises and deliver trade justice to the world's poor, then in our generation, there is every chance that poor countries like Tanzania will be upstanding and on the road to being totally self-sufficient. I am even more convinced of the need for the G8 to stick to the promises of Gleneagles. Aid does work, it does get through, and it can make an incredible difference. I've seen children being taught, learning to read and write, and they're doing it because we put pressure on our government to deliver the aid.'

In an interview with the BBC's Andrew Marr while in Tokyo (standing in a field), he also talked more fully about his 2007 Tanzanian trip and what it meant to him: 'I'm always slightly made uneasy by the fact that people's first response to all these issues or the central issue of the fact that half the world has not enough and the other half has too much, is to reach way down the agenda for things like, "Oh there's a lot of corruption out there". Africa is not one country; it's a collection of many countries. Obviously we won't be giving Robert Mugabe any money and no one suggests that we should. In corrupt countries we would, we would strive to deliver the money directly to civil society organisations or directly to schools and clinics. It's a bit like saying we're not going to give Belgium any money because Holland's such a mess. And indeed, obviously if it were about Holland, we wouldn't be having this conversation. The planes would already be in the air.'

On his involvement with the G8 summit, he added: 'I don't have any serious plans to personally lobby anyone; I don't think I'll be allowed that close. And if people are concerned about the general state of the world and the financial situation and rising food prices, and of course, climate change, what we at Oxfam are urging the leaders to do is to make poverty central to all of those discussions because it is, it informs everything and the poor are the first people – guess what – to suffer from climate change and the effects of it and indeed from, obviously, from rising food prices. So, any kind of possible recession is best viewed through a global perspective and including the poor of the world. Because that is part of the solution.'

He was grateful to return home from his Japanese

trip in the knowledge that he had had a good enough break from filming – two months before work on his new film, *Wild Target* – to rest up. Sadly, this was time he would spend very much as a bachelor.

In July that year, he would receive another nomination. Not for his acting, but as one of the country's 'Groovy Old Men', a title conjured up by the *Independent* newspaper. Bill was named among the likes of David Bowie, Trevor Eve, Bryan Ferry and Leonard Cohen. In the article, the *Independent* described the 'GOM' as, '...in their £120 Paul Smith shirts, their huge, converted warehouse apartments in Bermondsey, their iPods full of The Fratellis and Bloc Party alongside Springsteen and Dylan, their Gillette clippers for disposing of nasal and aural hair, their MySpace entries, their discreet trips to the chemist for Viagra, Cialis and vitamin supplements, their insouciance before the raised eyebrows of women and the alarm of their offspring.' While Bill might have agreed with some of it, he would certainly have disagreed with most of it!

Chapter Eleven

Behind the Scenes

While all appeared well on the professional front, in private, Bill was forced to deal with separation from the 'extraordinary woman' who had been his saviour. Diana Quick – 'the love story of my life' – quietly moved out of the couple's north London home. For some time, the relationship had been foundering, not helped by the enforced absences caused by Bill's acting schedule. Indeed, he was still playing the bohemian, with no real feeling of being 'at home'. His London property might be worth over £1.5m, but he rents it. As un-materialistic as ever, he doesn't believe in purchasing furniture either.

Being away for up to six months at a time took its toll on any quality time Bill and Diana might have enjoyed together. In between her own acting work, she was spending more time at their Suffolk home. Separations that once kept their passion alive were now destroying it. The words Bill had once spoken about the unique relationship that he and Diana shared when they first got together now came back to haunt him: 'Since then, we have had typical actors' lives. We have had separations for work reasons. She turned down a lot of work when our daughter was little to be around. But those separations have probably stopped us getting sick of the sight of each other. It has kept it fresh.' Long ago, the two considered the idea of getting married. It wasn't something one did when they were young, explained Bill, and even now, with marriage coming back into fashion, legalising their relationship was no longer important. Bill said: 'I don't worship in any particular establishment, and the legality of it is not a concern, so it was never an imperative for us. There were times when Mary got wind that there was such a thing as weddings and we hadn't had one. She figured she might lobby for that, just in terms of getting a new frock and some cake and a day out. Children like weddings.'

Diana had always maintained a silence about her relationship with Bill, once stating: 'We have this policy of not talking about each other. I'm very proud of him, but I just don't want to discuss our life together.' Time they should have perhaps spent talking over their problems just never materialised. When they did meet, it often ended in bitter rows rather than trying to figure out what had gone wrong. Bill's dedication to his work could be most to blame. That, and the failure to keep on working at a long-term relationship that desperately needed it. Diana found it hard to cope with his loner tendencies and insecurities, neither of which had really abated, despite his undoubted success. 'I was disabled by self-consciousness when I was young and I have good days and bad days now,' Bill once admitted. Then there were his idiosyncrasies. His refusal to celebrate Christmas meant a miserable time for Diana; she often spent the holiday travelling with Mary because Bill did not recognise that time of year as being worthy of a break.

Diana once said: 'Physical passion was important to me when I was younger, but I find I don't really need it in my life any more. Once in a while the chance to have an affair comes my way, but it doesn't tempt me.' At the same time, Bill admitted his fame meant that he was regularly propositioned by women – one of whom jumped out of a London taxi dressed in a leather cat-suit and invited him home!

The separation was reported in the *News of the World* on 24 August 2008 and shocked friends and family – even Diana's sister Julie did not know until she read the newspaper reports. The split was 'devastating', according to a source quoted there: 'Everyone thought their relationship was rock solid but Diana wants nothing more to do with him. Bill's career has taken off over the last few years, turning him into a huge star, but it's been a different story for Diana, as it's harder for older actresses to find work. The pair have lived increasingly separate lives, and she's been left on her own.' It appeared to be the end of the relationship between the woman Bill always referred to as his 'wife' and the man Diana described as her 'POOSSLQ' – Person Of Opposite Sex Sharing Living Quarters. Sharing, but no longer really caring, was what it seemed to have amounted to. Diana finally left after what should have been a make-or-break meeting ended with Bill unable to agree to an ultimatum over their relationship.

Signs that all was not well had already been noticed. Although Bill accepts that he has to do interviews, he doesn't really enjoy them because he hates talking about himself. He will happily report on the making of a film or play, but personal probing makes him feel deeply uncomfortable. He once said: 'I don't know how other people perceive me. We all have slightly the wrong idea about each other and that's fine. I used to concern myself that people would go away with the wrong idea about me – but I know they already have the wrong idea to some degree.'

Asked about his relationship, he became nervous, going through the motions of touching wood, while saying that everything at the moment was fine. There were also the tell-tale signs that he shows when he is uncomfortable in a situation: he performs a kind of teeth-grinding motion, moving his mouth sideways as if trying to keep his true feelings in. Sharp-eyed cinema fans would have noticed this trait in one particular scene in *I Capture the Castle* when his character, depressed author James Mortmain, talks about how he feels he has let the family down. In interviews, it is a sign that he is annoyed or irritated by the person questioning him. Naturally, being asked about the woman he has described as the 'love story of my life' was exceptionally painful and he was unwilling to reveal details of something so deeply personal.

It became a habit of his to conduct interviews in hotel rooms with the curtains closed, as if retreating from an outside hurt. Bill said he likes to see, 'the shapes on the drapes more than the horizon. I dig the horizon if I'm out walking, but if I'm in a room I like it to be lamp-lit.' He keeps the shutters closed at his London home because, 'I can never think of a good reason not to.' The closest he could come to acknowledging that maybe, just maybe, he was coping was to say: 'I'm pretty OK, like everyone. It's a funny old world... I pretty much worry about everything. But lately I'm working on swinging on down the avenue and seeing what gives. I have good days and bad days.' However, he admitted to becoming obsessed with work – at the time he had 7 films lined up within 12 months.

Four days after the announcement, Bill and Diana were seen, arm-in-arm, coming out of Scott's restaurant in Mayfair. Strangely, although they were no longer together, it was the first time they had been photographed in public for over two years. They issued a statement saying: 'Bill and Diana separated amicably eighteen months ago. They remain great friends.' The involvement of a third party was strongly denied and Diana was still wearing the ring that Bill had given her many years before, which she describes as 'her most treasured possession', along with the rings given to her by her daughter Mary and her mother.

A friend, quoted in the *Daily Mail*, blamed Bill for the couple's problems: 'I suppose you could call it a delayed mid-life crisis. After years of muddling through, he found huge success pretty late in life and he hasn't dealt with it especially well. He's been working himself silly and it's not good for him. He neglected Diana for years and I think she finally got sick of it.'

The same report stated that Bill's lifestyle had changed dramatically when he made it big, but it is hard to accept the following quote as his genuine idea of a good day. Anyone who knows him would suggest, perhaps, that it was said very much tongue-in-cheek: 'I'd go to watch David Beckham and Michael Owen play for Real Madrid, then go to a supper club, where Rachael Yamagata would be playing and singing. Then I would have a private plane take me to the Ritz in Paris, where I would stay in the Coco Chanel suite.'

A more average day would either be rising incredibly early, around 4.30am, or incredibly late if he has been up the night before watching football on television: 'The most precious time in the day is the first hour of the morning with a cup of tea, especially when I am filming. If I have a 5.30 a.m. call, then I like to get up at 4.30 for my tea and to read. Even four hours of uninterrupted novel reading isn't as special as that time. I make a mean *Haricots Blancs avec Sauce des Tomates* on toast with judicious use of Marmite. I like dessert to consist of hard Rowntree's fruit gums out of the box. Or I might indulge in a Lion Bar.'

Whatever the time, he will sit at the table with his hands wrapped around a cup of Yorkshire tea and just think. There will be breakfast at a local café (he dislikes smart restaurants and once refused lattes and espressos at a West End eaterie in favour of a pot of boiling water, to which he added his favourite Yorkshire Gold teabags, produced from the pocket of his elegant trousers). He also likes coffee, admitting to being in 'caffeine management', but gave it up in January 2009, preferring to be addicted to tea as it did not seem as serious an addiction as coffee. The rest of his meals comprise 'lots of fruit'.

Once he got over his sugar obsession, Bill tried to sustain a healthy diet: 'I tend to gorge, so to be free of it is marvellous. It also means I eat lots of fruit, which I never used to. And it means I am hungry, properly hungry, when I'm supposed to be. So I don't snack. God, I sound so marvellous! I don't have a strict regime, but I do a bit of exercise and I try not to put things in my body that might hurt me.' In fact, his real diet is very much that of a bachelor in a bedsit. He prefers sandwiches in the evening – with tuna melt and cucumber being his favourite – or baked beans on toast (with Marmite underneath, a nostalgic touch from childhood).

Bill even 'smuggles' Marmite through various airports on his foreign filming jaunts, admitting: 'I never know if it's legal or not. The sign says, "have you got any foodstuffs on you?" and I lie.' He also likes cheese on toast with the 'vital ingredient' of Worcestershire sauce. His grandmother used to make this special 'Welsh Rarebit' and he has always loved it: 'Comfort food? I don't understand that. Is there such a thing as discomfort food?'

A dish of corned beef, new potatoes, peas and brown sauce is another childhood favourite, which he still savours: 'I love the coldness of the beef against the hotness of the potatoes and the peas just set it off.' There was a time when he would knock back lots of ice-cold milk, but he has since given that up: 'Now of course I don't do it. Who drinks milk? It seems so reckless these days...'

One dish from schooldays, which he cannot bear to look at today, is semolina. It reminds him too much of the unhappy experience when he was 11 and in hospital, having his appendix out: 'They gave me semolina. I'm squeamish – words like "soggy" freak me out – and semolina didn't look like anything you were supposed to put in your mouth. The nurse left it there for hours right in front of my nose to try and force me to eat it – I've never forgotten it.'

Bill can cook, however – he can even make a Sunday roast, if he has to. But he doesn't. Anyway, that would mean having to turn a meal into a social event. Not his style. And filming commitments mean he has little time for entertaining at home or indeed just sitting around, having 'normal' meal-times: 'When I am at home, I'm often filming, so I only have a few hours to eat, sleep and learn lines.'

Most of his dining is done at hotels and restaurants. His favourite is The Wolseley on London's Piccadilly and the celebrity haunt, The Ivy: 'I love the atmosphere and the general terms of engagement. Everybody is pleasant and the service is impeccable.' When eating locally, close to his north London home, he prefers to visit the Thai restaurant, Charuwan – 'a superior place.' There, he always orders the same dish of stir-fried beef with chilli, green beans, Thai basil and pak choi. Bill orders this with such regularity that the staff don't offer him a menu anymore.

He once commented: 'I like places where you can dine on things like Arbroath smokies with eggs and colcannon [mashed potato with cabbage]. I also like places where the service is relaxed, but efficient. When on location you tend to eat out a lot as a group. After a bit I find myself getting phobic about anything "on a bed of" – I get to the stage of simply longing for an egg on toast. "Crushed new potatoes" marked a particularly low point in my relationship with menus.'

He once gave an insight into his somewhat lonely dining and domestic state when he admitted that although Diana was a great cook, she was not often at home either when the two were a couple: 'We don't have that kind of regular life where you come home and have your dinner...'

If ever the occasion arose when Bill could fulfil his 'fantasy dinner party' dreams, his guest list would comprise Barcelona footballer Ronaldinho, country singer Shelby Lynne, singer/actor Gary Kemp and his wife Lauren, Sir Alex Ferguson, Aretha Franklin and his acting friends, Michael Gambon, Gene Hackman, Christopher Walken and Dame Judi Dench. Walken is a special hero of Bill's – he has admired the actor most of his life: 'I think he is a brilliant man – he makes you laugh, he makes you smile, he breaks your heart, he's everything, fabulously glamorous, attractive and deeply clever. I really, really admire him.' The two have never actually met, but Bill is happy with that, saying he wouldn't know where to put himself if he did encounter Walken because he is so 'utterly enthralled' by him.

His days at home in London include a stroll to a bookshop and music store – Bill does not own a car and never takes the Tube. Evenings, and some mornings too, 'just listening, like meditation', are spent listening to music. There was Bob Dylan of course, 'the single most important artist in my life', the Rolling Stones and The Who. It's not commonly known, but Bill is also a big fan of American black soul music – 'my first big enthusiasm' – and he listens to artists such as Marvin Gaye, Aretha Franklin and Otis Redding: 'I used to joke that I only listen to Bob Dylan, the Rolling Stones and Marvin Gaye if I have people over, just to be sociable.'

He has met Mick Jagger, but not Keith Richards: 'I don't know what I'd say to either of them. I'd probably just kneel down and say, "thank you very much". I would do something embarrassing and I am best protected from it.' It is his obsession with music that has him buying the same album several times. He once bought five copies of a Van Morrison album.

Then there is the walking of his dogs, Tibetan terrier Nellie and rescue mongrel Smokie – a time he also uses as 'thinking time.' He loves to wander and treasures periods of solitude. He is not an extrovert and in social situations, 'always feels slightly disarmed.' One *Sunday Times*' interviewer described Bill as, 'the sort of solitary person who is working hard not to seem solitary and is envious of those who can interact.' His own doubts of self-worth – or indeed that anyone should seek his presence – were neatly summed up by him: 'I have difficulty persuading myself that I'm on a guest list.'

After news of Bill and Diana's split became public, some said he seemed almost relieved that now all he had to be anxious about was his work. When not working, he can become a virtual hermit, not seeking company or even making phone calls: 'It's a bad habit and I regret it. I'm always grateful when people call me – I have some sort of resistance to making arrangements, I've just never been good at making those calls myself.'

He will answer the phone, however – his deep-rooted insecurity that it will never ring with work offers ensures that. And he hates not working. 'I don't relax,' he admits. 'I think it's bad for you. I'm too anxious and too wired, I just want the phone to ring.' When he isn't working, he often seems to go on a sort of autopilot of aloneness. It's a trait that worries friends like David

Hare and his fashion designer wife, Nicole Farhi, who desperately try to prise him out of his home. Said a friend: 'Bill is sparkling company when he is out, but he prefers to be alone and most of the time he is resolutely solitary. We worry about him.' His good friend Stephen Poliakoff, who directed Bill in *Gideon's Daughter*, accused him of withdrawing from the world. 'Well, I don't think so – I get the information I need and if there is something really pressing, someone will alert me to the fact,' Bill insisted.

An insight into his attitude was given during an interview with musiccomh.com, when he was asked what he would do on learning that the world was about to end. Just how would he spend those ten minutes or so? Would he call a loved one? No. Seek the company of another? No. Pray? Definitely not! 'I'd put the kettle on for a cup of Yorkshire tea (they owe me money!), I'd put on a Stones' album (don't ask me which one, or if you forced me, *Sticky Fingers*), then I would phone my dogs and see how they were doing and say goodbye, formally, and then I'd reach for some poems, *The Complete Works of Harold Pinter*, and I would read myself a couple of Harold's poems – which always cheer me up – and then I'd check my hair! You know what I'm saying? You don't want to go with your hair a mess! And then I'd kick back and relax.'

The wild days are long gone. Bill now prefers an early night and a good book: 'I've been around too long to be able to manage to go out partying in the evenings and work as well. I can't do both any more. I used to do a full day's filming and then hit the street, but after a 14-hour day, I just feel my time is too precious. I like to be in bed by 11pm, even though I often indulge in a meal out by myself with a book. Restaurants and taxis are really my only extravagance – I don't do drugs or anything else that's expensive.'

Bill Nighy is a complex man with many idiosyncrasies and he cannot be easy to live with. He is, for instance, a 'packaging freak', saying that, 'when people give me gifts and the packing is particularly superior, they remain unwrapped because I know whatever they contain wouldn't give as much satisfaction as the packaging does.' Then there is the ongoing, ever-present, crippling discomfort with his body, too. It has such a vice-like grip on his self-image that he always showers in the dark: 'I'm not particularly keen on the sight of myself, to a kind of extreme degree. I know it's nuts because I'm perfectly acceptable-looking but it is a reality. It's not modesty, it's not coyness, it's not affectation. I wish it were because it's caused me an enormous amount of trouble.' And while not particularly house-proud, he does have to have some order: 'I never do anything useful, like clean up, but if there's a magazine that's slightly not on top of the magazine beneath it, I have to go over there and sort it out. I'm a very good straightener.'

Asked by a journalist if he had suffered a mid-life crisis, Bill replied: 'I think I have, but no one took a blind bit of notice! It wasn't any different from my early-life crisis or all my later ones, it so resembled a normal day.'

Would he ever be able to change? 'Probably not, it's getting late in the day,' he confessed. 'I don't know how other people perceive me. We all have slightly the wrong idea about each other, and that's fine. I used to concern myself that people would go away with the wrong idea about me – but I know they already have the wrong idea to some degree.'

So, what does he enjoy? He is a very adept texter (of the two-thumbs kind), but he does not have a computer and rarely watches television, apart from football – 'When I'm away, I find the Fox soccer channel and I watch the English Premiership; I love all of it.' But he does, of course, love films. Here, courtesy of the Rotten Tomatoes website, are his favourites:

Bowfinger: 'Steve Martin and Eddie Murphy make me laugh out loud. Eddie Murphy makes me laugh, generally speaking. Steve Martin makes me laugh – I love him with all my heart – and the combination was just beautiful. At the end, when Eddie Murphy begins to believe the things that have been weirdly happening to him are in fact true, and that he might save the universe, it always makes me laugh out loud. I love the fact that he comes in and says to Steve Martin at one point, "Guess who I had intercourse with last night?" – which always makes me smile.'

He lists Steve Martin as one of his first choices to star alongside, given the chance: 'If he ever got on the phone, then it would take me no time at all to say yes. I am so grateful there is someone like him. He has made a couple of films which are in my top all-time favourites – as well as *Bowfinger*, there is *Roxanne* and *The Man with Two Brains*. Eddie Murphy, too – I think he is absolutely marvellous. I saw him at the Golden Globes and nearly approached him, but didn't. He is a fabulous talent.'

Performance: 'It's predictable, but *Performance*, the Donald Cammell movie, contains one of the great cinema performances from James Fox. There's a scene where he's getting ready, and there's a bit where he arranges his Playboy lighter, and the magazines, and the ashtray, perfectly symmetrically aligned on the coffee table, the funky coffee table. And then he gets his tie and his shirt absolutely fabulous, and the hair is right – and I love it with all my heart, and I love the whole movie, and I love him in it... And then, he looks in the mirror and says: "I am a bullet." And my heart goes boom. Mick Jagger is in there too, giving a very good performance, and I know that by heart too. The soundtrack is epic, it's beautiful, including a great Mick Jagger song called "Turner's Song: Memo from T", which is a great, great song with some beautiful lyrics. It's just a film that I have a soft spot for.'

Mississippi Burning: 'It's a movie where I have to stay there, just to get to the bit where Gene Hackman creeps up behind the bigot in the barbers and takes the cut-throat from the barber's hand and continues the shave. The story is such a big and important story. I was asked recently, along with dozens of other people, to pick one film, by the BFI, to mark the 75th birthday of the British Film Institute. Which film would you leave for succeeding generations? There are many great art films but I chose *Mississippi Burning* because I figured that I would try to be responsible. I thought I could either be hip or responsible, and actually stick to the brief, and by succeeding generations, I assumed they meant the youth, young people, and I thought: "What's the biggest issue in the world?"

'Apart from the way that drugs fuck everybody up, racism is the biggest thing. The newspaper is basically the story of what racism does, whether it's religious prejudices or tribal prejudices, or colour prejudice or whatever the fuck it is, but I think it's the single most destructive element in our world and *Mississippi Burning* is a beautiful story of great courage. It shows individual and collective courage in that area, about people who took it on in a landmark situation and started to make great change possible. It's got one of the great cinema performances of all time, not that I'm given to superlatives, despite it being the second time I've said that, which is Gene Hackman. I could watch Gene Hackman all day long; he's one of the people I most admire.'

Punch Drunk Love: 'This is absolutely perfect. It is one of the most beautiful, fabulous performances. I adore

Punch Drunk Love and I can almost recite it to you. It was on TV on a loop for a while, and it's like *The Godfather*, you hit that film on TV and you stay there. There aren't many, but you just stay there, thinking, "I could keep flipping, but there's not actually going to be anything better than this," and it doesn't matter that you've seen it sixteen times – you just dig it because it's such high quality.

'I think Adam Sandler and Emily Watson are completely marvellous in it, and I didn't know anything about Adam Sandler, I've never seen any of his other films, so I've only seen him in this. I love Paul Thomas Anderson and I think it's my favourite of his films. Everyone is fabulous in it. It is one of the wittiest and cleverest expressions of love I have ever seen. It is possibly a controversial thing to say, as his other films are, perhaps, hipper, but I love the fact that it's this fucked-up love story. I love it stylistically, the jokes, the visual attitude of it and those funky links that he does. I love the apparent arbitrariness of the plot, which hinges on the fact that you get free air miles with a particular brand of chocolate pudding, and I love the way it dovetails at the end. Everyone in it is magnificent, including Philip Seymour Hoffman, who's in *The Boat That Rocked* and who is beautiful in *Punch Drunk Love*.

'Adam Sandler gives one of the greatest light entertainment performances I've ever seen. It's a submerged light entertainment, it's so integrated, so authentic in terms of naturalism, that you surprise yourself by laughing, because it's so deadpan, so undercover in terms of comedy, and that's my favourite thing of all time, the highest level. For the first twenty minutes, you think you're in art-movie hell, but you're not, so don't panic. What most of my favourite films have in common is that they all make me laugh. And they all give me hope. You feel considerably better when you come out of the cinema than when you go in. You have insight, you are thrilled, you think everything might just be worth it...'

Bringing up Baby: 'With Cary Grant and Katharine Hepburn, I have to stay there. I don't know how people can act that quick. I'm a big fan of quick acting, and I'm going to try to build it into my career from now on – I've been thinking about it for a while now. I think in the old days, everybody used to act really quickly because Hollywood was built by theatre people. And I don't believe that cinema is a non-verbal medium, I believe people should have T-shirts made with, "Cinema is a not a non-verbal medium," because I don't know how that entered the language – it's from people who can't write, presumably. I don't believe that, in some way, having a theatrical background should exclude you from the movies, which was a fashionable thing in the 1970s. It's ludicrous, given that Hollywood is built by mostly European theatre people. You can't speak any quicker than Cary Grant speaks in most of his movies – it's really cool – and everybody gets everything, nothing misses. I love to watch those two together because they're dry, they're witty, they're funny and it's romantic, and they get together in the end.

'And I always remember watching *Mean Streets*, which was the first time I ever heard a Stones song in a movie. It was on the jukebox in the club, *Jumpin' Jack Flash* was the song, and it was shocking that the Rolling Stones would allow one of their songs to be in a movie. But Scorsese has always had them in there – he's a man of taste. They have a long relationship, because the Stones don't let just anybody use their songs, you'd never get a Rolling Stones' song in your movie.

'I also enjoyed *Shine a Light* – I thought it was wonderful. I loved the guests, Christina Aguilera, my God! What is that? She's got so much talent, she's so brilliant, and she looks so beautiful. You can see Mick's face – he looked like he was so happy. Not only is she sensationally beautiful, glamorous and sexy, but also she can really, really, really do it, and the two of them pumping out that song was just beautiful. I've never seen a man look more happy or more grateful than Jack White, standing there singing *Loving Cup*. If you ever want to see a portrait of a young man looking as happy as it's possible for a young man to look, check out Jack White in *Shine a Light*.

'At one point, they've both got a microphone – Mick's got one, he's got the other, but he can't bear it – he rushes over and shares a mic with Mick because you know he wants to be able to say, "I shared a mic with Mick." Then, at the end he shakes everybody's hand, Charlie, Keith and everybody, and if he was a dog he'd wag himself to death. If he'd had nine tails, it wouldn't have been enough.

'I'd also have said *The Godfather*, because it is one of the greatest films ever made, but it's too obvious! I also like to watch *Sign o' the Times* with Prince because he does the splits whilst playing the guitar and comes back up on the backbeat, and anyone who can do that is good enough for me. Also, *The Last Detail*, with Jack Nicholson and Randy Quaid, which is a marvellous movie, and all those 70s movies, like *Dog Day Afternoon* with the young Al Pacino. If you haven't seen it, check it out. *The Servant* with James Fox and Dirk Bogarde is another great English film, that if you want to see two halves of the 60s British films, check out *Performance* with James Fox and check out *Le Serpent* with James Fox, and then you get a pretty good idea, both ends of the spectrum.'

Despite personal turmoil, there was reason to celebrate in 2008. Anyone who knows Bill is aware of his fierce loyalty and support of friends and favourite causes so it was no surprise that, despite his heavy workload, he had taken time out to team up with fellow actors Timothy West, David Suchet, Dame Judi Dench and Prunella Scales for some worthy nostalgia. Hearing that Newbury's Watermill Theatre, the venue where their stage careers began, was under threat of closure, Bill had joined a campaign in August 2006 to raise

£1m and urged everyone to support the appeal. It was a last-ditch bid to save the theatre, which first launched its fund-raising appeal in June 2005 with a target of £3m.

Incredibly, and with eternal thanks to more than 4,000 foundations, friends and fans, this target was reached in October 2008. Chairman of the Save the Watermill Appeal, Ralph Bernard, described the success as, 'an extraordinary time in the theatre's history.' The cash enabled the theatre to be bought by the specially formed Watermill Theatre Limited for £1.6m, with the rest of the funds raised spent on major refurbishment of the 25-year-old building.

No one was more delighted than Bill: 'It is such wonderful news that the appeal to Save The Watermill has reached its target. Now other young actors, directors and creative teams can benefit from the same encouragement and support that I received, when I worked there in my first ever job. Theatre is crucial to our development as a society and to have avoided the catastrophic loss of one as important and as beautifully appointed as The Watermill is a marvellous thing in the modern world.'

He is also involved in The Factory, a company dedicated to a 'continuous and evolving exploration' of the theatrical art form. It provides a forum for a network of artists and not only puts on classic, contemporary and debut productions, but also has a workshop for actors, directors and writers.

Bill's work schedule was still hectic. On 17 September

he started filming *Wild Target*. Directed by Jonathan Lynn, it is the tale of a hit man, who falls in love with his next victim. Some of his old friends also starred: Emily Blunt, Rupert Everett, Rupert Grint, Martin Freeman and Eileen Atkins. Shooting took place in London and also meant another return to the Isle of Man for Bill.

He was back working with director Stephen Poliakoff in a World War Two thriller titled *Glorious 39* alongside Dame Maggie Smith, Romola Garai, Julie Christie, Jeremy Northam and *Dr Who* star, David Tennant. The film was shot in London and Norfolk and is a period piece set in 1939 as war looms over Europe.

One of his last projects of 2008 was a BBC Radio 4 broadcast of another in the Charles Paris' Mysteries, *The Dead Side of the Mic*. It went out over three broadcasts on 10 December and in this story, Paris lands himself a job at the BBC Drama Company with murder stalking the halls of Broadcasting House. Bill was back alongside his radio stalwart in the series, Nicky Henson, together with Suzanne Burden, Tilly Gaunt, Emily Raymond and Chris Pavlo. That same month, he made a return to Radio BBC 7 in *The Entertainer*, a touching analysis of three generations of a family after the Second World War.

He also provided the voice of the 'Ringmaster' in the animated feature, *A Fox's Tale*, about a young fox called Little Jack (voiced by Freddie Highmore), who lives happily with his family in the forest until his father is trapped and forced to work in a travelling circus. Little Jack calls on a disabled boy and the circus owner's daughter to help him free his parent. Miranda Richardson and Sienna Miller also provided voices for the film, which was released the following year.

He resurrected his character of vampire king Viktor for *Underworld: Rise of the Lycans*, directed by Patrick Tatopoulos and released simultaneously in the UK and America on 23 January 2009. Filming took place between January and May the year before and strangely, although this was the third *Underworld*, it was the 'prequel' to the other two movies. His fellow cast members included Michael Sheen (Lucian), new female star Rhona Mitra as Sonja (described by Bill as 'brilliant and beautiful and lovely'), Steven Mackintosh as Tannis, Kevin Grevioux as Raze and David Ashton as Coloman.

The story delves into the origins of the centuries-old feud between the aristocratic vampires known as death dealers and the werewolf Lycans. Young Lycan Lucian is the powerful leader who rallies the werewolves to rise up against Viktor, who has persecuted them for years. Lucian is joined by a secret lover – beautiful vampire Sonja, Viktor's daughter.

In an interview with the *Radio Times*, Bill proclaimed his fondness for the *Underworld* films and praised the commitment of the men behind them; Len Wiseman, Danny McBride and Richard Wright, adding that all three were 'deeply tutored in vampire lore.' He had no qualms about playing Viktor for a third time: 'I do like hissing. I like giving it a bit of vampire cat. When you get your fangs in – when you get your battle fangs in, I should say, because, as you probably know, there are two levels of fang. There is your usual street fang and then there is when you get engaged and they suddenly become much longer and fiercer. When you get your battle fangs in and hiss, I enjoy that. There was a scene the other day with Michael Sheen, where I don't think there was any dialogue. It entirely consisted of him roaring at me and me hissing back him. I do enjoy that stuff.

'The phenomenon of vampires has always appealed to me. Everyone kind of likes a vampire story because it could be true. There are those moments when you get another report of some remains found in Transylvania that indicate that perhaps it was possible in 1107 AD that there was a guy who existed purely on blood. It is almost true. It is just a funky kind of lore. The whole idea of them is great.'

He told the *Radio Times* that he wanted to give the character of Viktor his 'own spin' without making him 'too obvious': 'I hate to start talking like this because it sounds so pompous whenever you start talking about acting. A lot of the choices I make are based on what I don't want to be; it is just trying not to repeat stuff that is done elsewhere. It is like when people do Shakespeare. For generations, when people have been asked to do Shakespeare, they bend one leg, put their other hand on their sword, put their chin up slightly and start talking funny. It is like it is handed down in the DNA, it is really bizarre. It is to be resisted because it is not good for anybody and it is not good for business.

'Apart from that, I don't know what I drew on. They put me in a skirt, which always has a very profound effect on me. It is very liberating. I recommend it – except in the wet. The problem with genre movies is everything is wet, you forget that. So, when I said, "Yes, I will wear a full length velvet skirt," it sounded like a good idea until I got on set. The set looks perfectly alright now but as soon as you start shooting, the guys come in with the hoses and it starts dripping, so everything is wet all of the time. It is a vampire world and it is a castle, and you can't have a dry castle. It's got to be wet, so you end up with a very soggy bum. You don't need to know that detail, but now you do. It is a battle skirt, obviously. We should always preface the word "skirt" with the word "battle".'

In truth, he was none too thrilled with the 'savage' bits of his character. He simply doesn't do all-action heroes or any of that swashbuckling stuff. As for stunts, forget them! Stuntman Paul Shapcott took over in *Underworld*, 'when it gets physical.' Bill prefers to just 'be' in a film and act. He told interviewer Paul Fischer: 'I'm not mad about the action part of things. My action career, as you may have noticed, is – basically – the amount of action in my career is thin upon the ground, so I have no great enthusiasm. You know, if you show me a stunt, I want to lie down and go to sleep. I have zero interest in fighting, zero interest in horse riding. I have minus interest in anything to do with physical aggression. It just makes me – you know, it's like juggling. I don't mind if you can juggle or not, you know what I mean? In the same way as, I don't mind if you can blow up a building, I don't mind if you can jump off a flaming tower. I only like the bits in between. I like the bits where they talk, and where the story is told.'

He does not adhere to any form of misuse over one's physical abilities (well, now that he doesn't move every part of him about on stage or screen so much) and the idea of getting in a bust-up with another man abhors him. It's simply not his style: 'It is so ungentlemanly, one would ruin one's clothes. I've never hit anyone. Blokes fighting just look horrible. Their faces go funny, their bodies look stupid, they get dirty and their clothes don't look good any more. I spotted that quite early on. Apart from the fact that it hurts.'

Somehow you get the impression that Bill would be prepared to fight a duel, if such things still existed, though. Particularly if anyone's honour had been dented.

One again, the part called for a mega makeup job to create a character intended to be 1,000 years old. This was another occasion when Bill had 'nice men doing medieval things to you' – and everyone else refusing to eat lunch with him! He would, he admitted, have preferred just to step into a costume with a zip in the back, but had become fond of his character: 'I would love to have one in the hall, actually – if it had the right skirt on. I do enjoy the whole genre thing. It's something that came late in my career and unexpectedly, but I embrace it.'

So, did he find it difficult to get out of character at the end of the day? 'Actors always talk about taking their work home and I always think: "What are you on? You just turn it off. You are at work and then you go home." But maybe you should ask people's wives and families because they are best placed to know. I don't go back to the hotel and hiss at people, at least I don't think I do.'

The critics certainly enjoyed his on-screen hissing. 'Bill Nighy is a practiced and expected scene-stealer...' wrote Jesse Hassenger on Filmcritic.com.

Bill said that working with Patrick Tatopoulos was, 'Brilliant, completely brilliant... I could work with him for the rest of my life! If Patrick was the only director left in the world, I'd be happy. He was marvellous. He's courteous as anything, he's sharp as a tack; he keeps it simple so I can understand it... He's absolutely dead-on with the story. He's very sharp at tuning the performance, which largely consists of him saying, "For God's sake, take it down, Bill!" – or something like that. He's courageous enough to say what's needed to be said anytime and exemplary. I was very pleased to work with him and would love to work with him again.'

In short, he was delighted with his third *Underworld* movie: 'I love the whole vampire shtick. You know, if you're in the movie for a vampire werewolf movie, you'd have to go some to find anything as satisfying as this series, in my view. I like the character, and I was very happy to be in number three. I'm going to be even happier if there's a number four.'

Underworld: Rise of the Lycans went straight in at No. 2 at the American box office and was to gross $89,102,315 worldwide. Bill was happy with the project. And it gave him the chance to be horrible without anyone disliking him – which would upset him greatly: 'It's slightly more fun to play a nasty character, because in life you're not generally allowed to be nasty. And you can arrange your face in satisfyingly horrible ways. Playing the good person, there is a narrower range of facial work.'

Though a very public face, Bill does much in private that endears him to the public. Three students at Bridgwater College were stunned when he turned up there in February 2009 and asked them to help him make a promotional video. The film was for the White Ribbon Alliance Charity, which promotes healthy motherhood in the developing world. The students, Rich Hall, Jordan Hatton and Matt Ives, were called on to source props and generally help with the making of the film – including tea and coffee runs, which they didn't mind a bit!

It was made by local director Julien Temple and Bridgwater College was chosen for a scene in which Bill played a newsreader because it handily had a large blue screen, which was needed to recreate an earlier scene filmed at Downing Street with Prime Minister

Gordon Brown and his wife, Sarah. The scenes were shot in secret to avoid crowds arriving to stare at their acting hero. This suited Bill, who still can't come to terms with being recognised and being expected to react to fan worship: 'Most of the time, I just forget I'm supposed to be famous. I'll be standing in a shop and notice that someone is staring at me for longer than is strictly courteous. I think either my flies are undone or "Do I know you?" You forget, because it's not on your screen – it's on other people's screens. But that sort of attention doesn't alter the way you are – if it did, it could drive you mad. People I meet are generally very cheerful towards me. No one has hit me, although you never know. Someone might come up to me and say "Jesus, not you again!" before smacking me in the mouth. There's got to be someone out there who can't tolerate me.'

It was later announced that he was one of several British actors being asked to donate one per cent of their wages during the first three months of 2009 for the UK charity, Comic Relief. Described by Comic Relief, an organisation close to his heart, as 'a unique initiative', the request was to culminate in 'Red Nose Day' on 12 March and Bill, together with fellow actors James McAvoy and Natascha McElhone, made a three-minute promotional film about the project, *Talking On the Tough Stuff*.

Ever dapper, the idea of being 'over casual' appalls Bill and he feels most comfortable in expensive jackets. He was still bemused to win what was not so much recognition for appearing in a film, but for his appearance in March 2009. He was voted third Best Dressed Man by *Esquire* magazine, pipped to first position by Prince Charles – who impressed with his double-breasted suits – and pint-sized comedian, 78-year-old Ronnie Corbett, who almost unfathomably won praise for his Argyle sweaters. Newly installed US president Barack Obama, 47, was praised for being a model of how to dress in 'tough times'.

This made Bill smile, as he once said there are only two men in the world who look good in shorts and Obama was one of them. You would never catch Bill in shorts. Not only would it betray his image of a well-turned out English gentleman – 'summer trousers are cooler, anyway' – but would, he says, necessitate smearing copious amounts of sun tan lotion on his very English, white legs: 'I go pink and septic in the sun if I don't smear,' he admits.

The other nominee was actor Brad Pitt – 'he is also the only man who can dignify a toga. You are never going to see me in a toga; I would rather starve than do toga parts. Yes, it's ruled out Julius Caesar, but then I've retired from Shakespeare.' As for the idea of sporting a tracksuit, Bill almost keels over at the suggestion. Still, he would have been devastated to be included in the 'worst-dressed' list alongside Gordon Brown and Boris Johnson. He takes particular care with his clothes and wouldn't dream of being seen looking anything other than impeccably dressed. It was only words of reassurance from Richard Eyre that enabled him to change his strident view that a man of a certain age should always tuck his shirt into his trousers.

'My major crisis is that, as I get older, things overtake me,' he admitted. 'Wearing one's shirt outside of one's trousers, which is generally the territory of the younger man, is unsettling for somebody of my years. It was only when Richard, who is slightly older than me, said, "Hey, look!" because he wears his shirt out of his trousers, I was finally emboldened to do so. I really didn't want to, but I'm over that now, and I was one of the last people of my age still wearing Doc Martens. My wife once said, "If you put on a decent suit and then put on a pair of DMs again, I'm going to leave you." I always had one pair of shoes. I never got my head round two pairs of shoes, and I still haven't, really.'

He is also particular to the point of near obsession over the care of his *Esquire*-admired wardrobe of fine shirts, mostly light blue in colour, two Armani coats, tailor-made suits (he can get highly enthusiastic about cloth, trimmings and buttons and his tan John Lobb loafers from Jermyn Street). Despite pleas from those trying to organise his career, Bill still refuses to carry a BlackBerry because this would ruin the line of his clothes: 'A BlackBerry isn't too good for the line of the trouser. And you can't wear it in your jacket, because what's the point of having a decent jacket if you're going to imbalance it with a Treo or whatever?' The idea of clipping it anywhere else horrifies him: 'I'd have to kill myself, actually. If you catch me with a pouch on my belt, shoot me!'

He also has a near obsession as to how his jackets should be buttoned up: 'Middle, always. Top, sometimes. Bottom, never!' Almost invariably, he leaves his shirt cuffs undone. He admits that being elegant at all times is a reaction to the move from his working-class background to the 'white-collar' job of acting: 'There is a certain genre of working-class actors who dress up to go to rehearsal and I'm one of them, and then they ask you to crawl around the floor and be a beaver or something!'

One observer considered that perhaps the insecure actor sees Dunhill, the maker of his £2,000 suits of armour, as a designer shield to boost his confidence. 'I can only really operate in a decent lounge suit,' Bill once said. 'I'm a fetishist for what I like to refer to as "the lounge suit". It amuses me that it's a suit you might wear "in the lounge", wherever that might be.'

To get him talking about his appearance is to get him to repeat his oft-quoted criticism about his body – 6ft 2in, somewhat gangly and thin, but certainly attractive to women: 'I like to wear a jacket because I don't like my shape. Even in the sun without a jacket, I feel lost.' Clothes must be dry-cleaned – 'if it stands still long enough, dry clean it!' – with the shirts neatly folded ready for packing. He also has an aversion to linen and will never wear it, not even in summer; he considers himself not 'man enough for silk' and refuses to wear the colours pink or yellow. 'Pink makes me uneasy. I am the wrong colour, and as a mousy-haired person, I fear yellow with all my heart. I will even try to avoid standing near anyone wearing it!'

Two years earlier, Bill finally accepted – and quite liked – the idea of wearing a tie: 'I never used to wear a tie when I was younger because you never got the girl, if you did. But I have taken up ties because it's my only opportunity for colour. I tend to be addicted to the same shade of navy blue, so a tie does help add a bit of colour. I haven't yet got any ties which are too loud colour-wise. It's early days and I am taking it one step at a time.'

You will never see him without his Eric Morecambe-style spectacles, especially when he has to read, and that can cause problems if his character is a 'no-glasses' one: 'I mean, I can play someone who doesn't wear glasses and I can see things in front of me, but when I have to read lines, well, that's when you have to start making it up!'

So, does he feel confident about anything to do with physical appearance? 'I'm very confident about... beauty. I'm confident about what I think is beautiful. I don't bother people about it much, but I do think I probably have unerring taste.'

A couple of months later, in June 2009, his 'unerring taste' earned him another award in the fashion stakes. He was voted seventh most stylish man in a list of 20, following a poll of 3,000 men run by luxury shirt company, Thomas Pink. Voters were also asked what they considered to be the most essential fashion items in a man's wardrobe (with a crisp white shirt coming first). The company said that all the nominated 'most stylish' men had been photographed 'numerous times' wearing white shirts, 'each adding their own individual stamp to this most timeless of looks.' Curiously, Bill does not favour white, preferring light blue instead. But an award is an award, and he did beat his *Pirates* co-star Johnny Depp (12th) and fellow young whippersnappers Justin Timberlake (17th) and Vernon Kay (20th). Just in case you're interested, top man was America's new president Barack Obama, who in just two months had risen through the ranks of dressing through 'tough times' to being a contender in trend-setting.

Incidentally, Bill also knows exactly how he likes women to dress. He likes to see them in suits, for a start: 'I love that Parisian look – a Chanel suit, kind of good as it probably will ever be... 9in heels, very little makeup, great hair. And I have this thing about a woman with no handbag. It's silly, but I associate that with Paris because when I was there as a kid, I used to see very elegant, smart women with their hands free. Just something about it is so thrilling. That's kind of it, for me.'

Bill is trusted in his fashion sense by the women he calls his 'two girls', Diana and daughter Mary, and while in New York, he went on a shopping spree for them.

That same month, he became a figurehead for the Royal Parks Foundation Half Marathon. Launched in October 2008, some 12,500 runners took part in the new London event. The novelty of the 13.1-mile route was that it took runners through the city's landmarks, taking in four royal parks, Buckingham Palace, the Houses of Parliament, Big Ben and Trafalgar Square, finishing in Hyde Park. The 2009 event took place on 11 October. Supporting it was just another of Bill's altruistic traits when it comes to things or people he cares passionately about. The Royal Parks Foundation raises funds for 5,000 acres of green space in London and in his otherwise frenzied life, Bill needs the calm of park environments: 'I rely on the presence of trees. I'm not quite a country boy, but I was born on the fringe of town, in Surrey, on the edge of the North Downs, so I'm accustomed to greenery. I live in London because I have had to professionally, but parks are invaluable. They are the lungs of our city.'

You won't find him jogging around London, but he is a keen brisk stroller and dog-walker: 'In the modern world, one needs to do something in terms of exercise because we don't do manual labour any more. With any kind of exercise, what I like is the reward. You get to feel much better and that's what keeps me coming back. The Half Marathon is a marvellous thing to do. It can only make you stronger and do you good. The parks provide a unique and beautiful experience, so people couldn't be running for a better cause. I wish everyone the best of luck.'

He was also keen to support the half marathon because it was raising money for 165 other charities too, including Unicef, the Blue Cross and Asthma UK.

At the same time, he upped his commitment to encouraging more foreign aid for teaching in impoverished countries. He recorded a personal message, which was included on DVDs of the Emmy award-winning, politically provocative film, *The Girl in the Café*. Copies were then sent to the US and targeted state members in Jersey in a bid to encourage the US to increase its overseas aid spending. On 20 July, Bill made an appearance at Oxfam's Marylebone High Street bookshop in London to publicise the charity's first Bookfest, aimed at encourage people to donate books to and buy from Oxfam shops.

The next month, it was announced that Bill was one again combining his love of books with a charitable cause. Together with the likes of Tom Stoppard, Stephen Fry, Jo Brand, Harry Hill and Nigel Slater, Bill allowed thoughts on what makes him happy to be included in *Modern Delight,* a charity book from Waterstone's, published on 10 September, to raise funds for Dyslexia Action and the London Library. Bill was also called on to contribute to another charitable book called *Inspired by Music*, sponsored by Starbucks and in aid of the Prince's Trust, for which celebrity ambassadors were ask to give an account of their favourite piece of music. No prizes for guessing which artist Bill chose. It was Bob Dylan and the track "Things Have Changed". Said Bill in the book (which was available from 10 July at Starbucks and some bookshops): 'The fact that I find this song inspiring could indicate that I am not in very good shape, given that it contains some grim observations of how bad things can get. What is uplifting, apart from its general brilliance, is that it is thrilling to know that you are not alone in these matters. It's also, as his songs often are, amusing. Any song containing the couplet "Feel like falling in love with the first woman I meet/ putting her in a wheelbarrow and wheeling her down the street" is more than fine with me. There is absolutely nothing wrong with this song. It is perfect. It obviously appeals to my isolationist tendency, but at least it swings. The refrain is an anthem for people like myself, who should probably get out more. ...'

Chapter Twelve

Still Rocking

Bill was back in rock'n' roll form for *The Boat That Rocked*, released in April 2009. He played Quentin, the owner and captain of a 1960s pirate radio ship operating offshore of Britain. For the part, he got to wear some psychedelic suits ('nothing is overstated in the film. People really did wear trousers that awful!'), joining a cast which included Philip Seymour Hoffman, Rhys Ifans, Nick Frost and Rhys Darby, playing pirate ship DJs. He was thrilled once again to team up with Richard Curtis for the 'unashamedly feel-good' film.

'If you want to see doom and gloom, don't go and see this one,' he proclaimed. 'Whatever else the film might be, it was mainly an excuse for Richard to play all the songs from that period – The Who, The Small Faces, The Kinks... He is a slave to them.' The background to Quentin was a little hazy: 'Richard and I did speculate that Quentin comes from an old traditional English family and he may have nicked a

Canaletto from the family stately home to finance the whole operation.'

The role called on him to dance – well, as best as he could – in front of the cameras. This is one particular performance that he hates to carry out in public, something he didn't enjoy, even when his teenage contemporaries were up there, giving it their all: 'I could never dance because I suffered from a mixture of reasonably profound self-disgust and intense vanity. I do actually like dancing, but I do it at home on my own.'

It helped that he remembered the age of pirate stations well (he would tune in to Radio Luxembourg in the very early days and latterly, Radio Caroline). In fact, this was the only chance for listeners to hear decent non-stop pop music as the BBC only played 'records' for two hours a week.

'The best thing about them was they had a good signal. Radio Luxembourg was great, but it would always drift off the signal – it wouldn't last you all the way through a song; it used you drive you insane. I would listen to it on a beautiful old wireless that I kept by my bed. It gave off heat,' he recalled fondly. 'You wait until your parents have gone to sleep, and then you turn on the radio. Radio Caroline was the first time you could get a signal and hear all of the new music and it was a kind of revolution, as people might remember. You went from your mum and dad's music which was basically people in their best clothes singing about the stars and the moon.' Like many of us, Bill too resented the fact that the music was regarded as being not 'legal'.

He said cynically: 'The government did this cool thing and made pirate radio illegal, which means you obtained outlaw status merely by tuning in.'

Five weeks of filming for *The Boat That Rocked* took place on board the *Timor Challenger*, a rescue boat anchored in Portland Harbour, Dorset, a year earlier in April 2008. The project caused a great stir, especially when news got out that Richard Curtis wanted locals to appear as extras. Under the headline 'CHANCE TO STAR IN $70M MOVIE', the *Dorset Echo* wrote: 'Starstruck movie-lovers could find themselves in front of the cameras in a blockbuster movie that is soon to be filmed on Portland... the new British film about rock 'n' roll on the high seas is expected to boost the local economy by more than £1 million.'

After auditions at Weymouth's Hotel Prince Regent, successful applicants received £80 a day for their work that May. It was the biggest event to hit the area for years, causing Jacqui Gisborne, communications manager for Weymouth and Portland Borough Council, to comment: 'This could be a once-in-a-lifetime opportunity to appear in a major British film. I would urge everyone to attend the casting and let's make it not just a British film, but a Weymouth and Portland film as well.'

'It was fun being on that boat,' recalled Bill. 'You'd think if you took a bunch of comic actors onto a boat and put a camera on them, there'd be blood on the floor, but there was a reckless absence of careerism of any kind. Richard Curtis is a very classy man and he creates a beautiful atmosphere. The collection of actors was a tribute to Richard and his script. It's marvellous to get that collection of people in one place at the same time and all very funny and very nice guys. We had a really nice time – I know they always say that, but we actually did have a marvellous time. We were floating on a boat off the coast of Dorset. We had a toastie machine, so we could have a toasted cheese sandwich any time we wanted. You could have anything you wanted – crisps, loads of crisps in different flavours – and you could dance all day. There were certain days we were required to simply dance. It turned into a sort of Elvis Presley movie, like a proper pop film or a pop video.'

He quipped that his experience as a sea monster – a reference to his Davy Jones' character – must have helped when *The Boat That Rocked* rocked just a little too much: 'I had an edge on the other guys because I'm a squid, as you know. Squids don't get seasick.'

Even before the film was released, there were some negative comments about Richard Curtis and his lightweight approach to storylines. This was rather unfair considering that he has been behind some of the best British feel-good films ever to come our way. At the end of the day, it is the public who queue up at the box offices and pay. Bill was quick to defend the work of his friend in interviews publicising his latest work: 'When people say that films are searingly honest, they are always searingly honestly grim. Well, this is searingly honestly cheerful, so it is honest. This is the cheerful bits. If you want to see the miserable, shabby, lousy, paranoid-making awful bits, check out someone else's movie. If you want to see searingly cheerful, groovy marvellous feel-good bits, come and see this.

'The absolute deal is that you feel an awful lot better when you leave the cinema than when you go in. Richard sticks to that and I admire him for that… this is shamelessly designed to make you laugh and make you feel fabulous. It has no other intention. Yes, I admit it. We did set out entirely to amuse you – there is no other agenda. We should have taken care of the other stuff, but we just didn't bother. We could have tried to do the responsible stuff, like undermine you and give you a biased view of how grim things can get, but we failed to do that and stuck entirely to the plan, which was to thrill you, play some of the great tunes and make you laugh…'

Despite this, *The Boat that Rocked* did not win the ecstatic acclaim that Richard Curtis' films usually enjoy. There were some good reviews, though, and one of the most glowing came from Nick Curtis in the London *Evening Standard*, who wrote: 'You've got to love Richard Curtis, actually. He's a one-man Ealing Studios, turning out a reliably funny, upbeat, and above all, commercial comedy every few years. It's fashionable to knock his optimistic films but we could all do with a bit of feel-good factor right now. *The Boat That Rocked* is Curtis's love-letter to the pirate radio stations he adored in his youth. It casts the cream of British comedy acting talent as the motley crew of *Radio Rock*, a shipful of reprobates broadcasting the devil's music to dolly-birds and schoolboys huddled around transistors, and flipping two fingers at the disapproving British authorities. Like all love letters, it's a bit gushy and over-the-top in places, but it also lifts the heart...'

London's *Time Out* review was not so good, however: '"The Ship That Sank" would be a more appropriate title for writer-director Richard Curtis's latest and most disappointing entertainment. It's a cripplingly self-conscious and self-satisfied tribute to the roistering last days of offshore British mid-'60s pirate radio before the meanies from the ministry pulled the plugs. It's also the kind of musical comedy where the actors seem to be having more fun than any audience could ever share. This overlong, poorly paced and slackly directed ship-bound farrago not only wastes its treasury of golden oldies – Hendrix, Kinks, Small Faces, etc. – but magically contrives to reduce the chaotic, creative spirit of the sexual and cultural revolution to a mere mechanical catalogue of trite and surprisingly sentimental sex-drugs-and-rock 'n' roll clichés, each fatally underlined by multiple and repetitive reaction shots. If there are compensations, they come courtesy of a few diverting performances.

'The movie's depressingly few incidences of genuine feeling come from Tom Sturridge, who is sweet and appealing as the public schoolboy taken under the wing of his godfather, ship's captain and Radio Rock boss Quentin, played by Bill Nighy as a self-parody in made-to-measure Regency-collared suits. Philip Seymour Hoffman does a turn as the radical, Emperor Rosko-like

DJ in rivalry with Rhys Ifans's self-serving immoralist Gavin. Elsewhere, pickings are slim: the talented Ralph Brown is wasted – he's cast as Wee Small Hours Bob, a misjudged amalgam, presumably, of "Whispering" Bob Harris and dysarthric Danny from *Withnail & I* – and the same is doubly true of such comic talents as Chris O'Dowd, Rhys Darby and Nick Frost.'

Bill was hurt about the less-than-enthusiastic reviews and some of the scathing comments about Curtis's frothy approach to film-making. The film was very successful in France and in Australia but as Bill admitted: 'It didn't go down well in England.' He felt there seemed to be some misguided relationship between critics and Curtis, saying: 'I don't get it. I think they have a specific problem with Richard. I should imagine there's a degree of resentment, but I don't read critics and concern myself with what they write. The world digs it profoundly and they turn up in their millions. The rest is a side issue.'

It had been a long time since he had appeared in something the public considered less than breathtaking, but generally, it seemed the critics were not so much dismissive of him, but of a film from a writer and director with such a previously high pedigree, who could seemingly do no wrong. Writing in the *Mail on Sunday*, Matthew Bond said: 'As a result, it's fair to say expectations come exceedingly high. And it's also fair to say those high expectations come nowhere as close to being met by a picture set in the so-called golden age of pirate radio in the mid-

Sixties. It always sounded an unlikely project for the rom-com king and so it proves.

'It's not funny enough, there's no great central love story and the editing, for so long one of the cornerstones of Curtis's richly deserved success, is terrible. The script is flabby, with scene after scene adding little to the story and some go on so long you forget why they started. As a result, the film weighs in at a grossly overweight 2 hours 15 minutes, half an hour longer than the flimsy material deserves.'

Bond did, however, have words of praise for Bill in what he called a 'misfiring film': 'Bill Nighy somehow manages to do a lot with very little material, and is funny without ever going over the top.'

The Boat That Rocked – released in America in November 2009 under the title *Pirate Radio* – was certainly not one of Curtis's great successes, grossing around £9m worldwide and it made Bill feel insecure to have appeared in the first-ever slightly under-performing Richard Curtis' film, but he was still realistic about the public's feelings of warmth for him. The best compliment you can give Bill is to suggest that the public will go and see a play or film simply because he is in the cast list. He still shrugs off too much praise, though: 'If I was younger, there might be a certain amount of heat attached to it, but I'm just an old lag, who people seem to like to see. I never expected any of it.'

His continuing insecurity was particularly marked in his interview with *Sunday Times* journalist Ariel Leve: 'I'm in a profession that couldn't be more uncertain. To make a living as an actor – I am clearly appreciative. I never expected to be on TV or in a film. It's all gravy to me. I'm never unaware of what's happened, and it means a lot to me that people like the stuff I've done. It's extraordinary. I don't take it lightly. I spent lots of years trying to retire from being an actor because I found it so difficult and alarming and because I was so self-conscious that I was disabled in professional terms.

'I used to stand around looking moody and hope that it would be mistaken for some type of interior landscape, and it was tough. And therefore any degree of acceptance is a tremendous thing for me. It is a big, big deal. I have to stop and take a second and draw attention to the fact that I'm a lucky man. In certain areas of my life, things have worked out. I mean, they are working out. The good news – and the bad news – is my progress so far has seriously exceeded any expectations I might have had. My expectations were exceeded a decade ago. And it got better. And then it got even better. It's breathtaking. There was a moment where I thought, I have everything I could ever want... But I'm not a film star – I'm that guy. It's just as it should be and it's just as I like it. It's a nice level of notoriety. People think, "Oh, is that Bill Nigby?"'

Throwing himself into other projects, he filmed *G-Force*, a half-live action, half-animated Disney film, in which he played one of the 'live' characters, Leonard Saber, with such luminaries as Nicolas Cage and Penélope Cruz providing the voices of Speckles and Juarez, respectively. The rather surreal story centred around a team of trained secret agent guinea pigs, who must take on a mission for the American government to stop an evil billionaire (Bill), who plans to destroy the world with household appliances. 'It was just a groovy job,' said Bill. 'It was the sweetest engagement and they looked after you really well.'

The part called for him to adopt an Australian accent – something he hadn't had to attempt since early acting days. He wasn't sure if he cracked it or not: 'What can I say? Obviously you'll be cringing in the aisles, but you're just going to have to open your heart and let me in and forgive me... I mean, I figure it's good otherwise I wouldn't have attempted it. But you may... you will almost certainly... Next time we meet, you'll be saying, "It was quite funny, but God, where did that accent come from?" The role had Bill once more taking on the challenge of having computer-generated images as his co-stars, causing him to comment: 'Mostly you end up talking to yourself, like a stupid person, or imagining that they are in the corner of the room or something.'. *G-Force* was released on 31 July 2009 and proved a summer holiday box-office success, taking $31,706,934 during its first weekend and $179,011,669 worldwide.

On 3 April 2009, Bill was back on BBC Radio 7 in *The Lotus And The Wind*, the third of John Masters' Savage family novels, in which Lt Robin Savage marches to the relief of Kabul. Also in the play, dramatised by David Wade and directed by Penny Leicester, were Juliet Stevenson, John Rowe and Nicky Henson.

That same month, it was announced that Bill would

contribute to a 160-page hardback work, *Inspired*, featuring celebrities from the worlds of film, TV, music and sport, all talking about how music has changed their lives. The book – published in July that year – also contained stories from young people supported by The Prince's Trust and included a foreword written by HRH the Prince of Wales.

On 2 June, Bill was heard in six repeat episodes of *Baldi*, the Franciscan priest and amateur detective, on Radio BBC7. Meanwhile, he awaited the release of *Wild Target*, in which he played Victor Maynard and starred opposite his friend, Emily Blunt: 'It's a remake of a French film about an anal, middle-aged lonely hit man who's never had a girlfriend. He's asked to kill a woman – played by Emily Blunt – and he can't pull the trigger. I can understand, because it's Emily Blunt.'

Socially, it was a quiet year for him and public appearances in London were rare. But he did make an outing to support close friend Nicole Farhi when she celebrated the 20th anniversary of her menswear business with a fashion show and private dinner at her showroom in Foubert Place. He also attended the première of *Young Victoria* – starring the girl he greatly admires, Emily Blunt – 'I usually feel a bit of a lemon at premières. I don't even like going on my own, but I am here to support Emily because she is someone I admire terribly. I do love period dramas, but I am really here to watch her. Emily is one of Britain's greatest talents, but she treats me with little or no respect, which is refreshing. She is incredibly charming, funny and glamorous with great depth. I'm excited for her.'

That May, he took time out to attend London's celebrated Chelsea Flower Show and had the honour of cutting the 40th birthday cake for David Austin English Roses.

If anyone had hoped for more intimate revelations from Diana Quick about her relationship with Bill, they would be disappointed. The autobiography she had spent so many years researching, *A Tug on the Thread: From the British Raj to the British Stage*, was published in May, but it gave little away. As the *Telegraph*'s Lynn Barber noted: 'There is no gossip. Nighy only appears as a name on her family tree and in one photograph; Finney and Cranham don't get a mention. The clue on the dust jacket is "a Family Memoir" and most of the book is devoted to Quick's nine years of research into her paternal ancestry in India. We get several chapters on the Indian Mutiny, a short history of dentistry from the 6th century BC (her father and grandfather were dentists), a chunk about Ayurvedic medicine and occasional lit crit excursions into Jean Rhys, Simone de Beauvoir and Ibsen's Ghosts. It has 12 pages of notes, five of bibliography, numerous footnotes and a glossary of Indian words, but says almost nothing about Quick herself.'

In June, Bill travelled to America and attended the second night of the Santa Barbara International Film Festival to present the 2009 Montecito award to Kate Winslet, star of *The Reader* and *Revolutionary Road*.

In the midst of all his offers of work, were a couple of plum roles that ultimately never came his way. Rumours that he would be the next Doctor Who in the BBC television series were soon scotched. And he was slightly miffed to learn that he was the 'only British actor who hasn't been asked to be in Harry Potter... David Yates, who directed *The Girl in the Café*, did the new one and has, apparently, agreed to do the one after that. I said to him, "So you have a part for me, mate?" And he just laughed.'

In early July 2009, one of Bill's cherished ambitions became a reality. He was granted his wish to appear in a Harry Potter film – *Harry Potter and the Deathly Hallows*. The project involved two separate films, which were scheduled for release on 19 November 2010 and 15 July 2011, in which he played the Minister of Magic, Rufus Scrimgeour. 'Getting the gig' as Bill once again described a plum role meant he had to actually had to sit down and read the Harry Potter books. 'It's rather like being in a Shakespeare that way, you know?' he said, adding that he was delighted to be working once again with David Yates and to be playing 'a minister, you know a heavyweight guy...'

As 2009 drew to a close and Bill celebrated his 60th birthday, there was much going on in both his professional and personal life. On 23 October, *Astro Boy* was released, in which he provided the voice for Dr Elefun. Set in a futuristic Metro City, it told the tale of its eponymous true hero with fun, action and computer generated imagery. The film was about a young robot created by a brilliant scientist called Tenma (voiced by Nicholas Cage). Astro Boy himself – voiced by Freddie Highmore – has super-strength and super-vision. Embarking on a journey in search of acceptance, he encounters many other colourful characters along the way. Ultimately, on learning his friends and family are in danger, Astro Boy marshals his awesome super-powers and returns to Metro City in a valiant effort to save everything he cares about and to understand what it takes to be a hero. It was something of a dark plot, but Bill joked: 'It's not like anyone is going to lose any sleep, I don't think. Mind you, I am the man that was carried out of Bambi! They had to put me to bed after the forest fire, so what am I saying?'

But what does it take to be a hero? 'Sometimes I ask myself the same question,' remarked Bill. 'You absolutely cannot plan your career in the movies. If you try, you'll be constantly frustrated. But every now and then, someone comes knocking on your door, not literally, but you receive an offer for a project – *Astro Boy*, *Valkyrie* – and you have to wonder. And you're thankful, because it turns out to be something rather stupendous.'

There was also Stephen Poliakoff's *Glorious 39*, a film set between present-day London and the idyllic Norfolk countryside in the lead up to the Second World War. At a time of uncertainty and high tension, it centred round the formidable Keyes family, who are keen to uphold and preserve their very traditional, English way of life. The eldest sibling Anne (Romola Garai) is a budding young actress, who is head-over-heels in love with Foreign Office official Lawrence (Charlie Cox). Anne's seemingly perfect life begins to dramatically unravel when she stumbles across secret recordings of the anti-appeasement movement. While trying to uncover the origin of these recordings, a tangled web of dark secrets begins to unfurl, culminating in the mysterious death of a dear friend.

As war breaks out, she discovers the truth and escapes to London to try to confirm her suspicions, but she is caught and imprisoned and only then does she finally begin to discover the true extent to which she has been betrayed. Also starring were Julie Christie, David Tennant, Juno Temple and Christopher Lee. Bill played Anne's father, Alexander.

The film hailed a return to the cinema for Poliakoff after an absence of 10 years and it was a project which especially satisfied him: 'I'm very excited to be making this film about a period that has always fascinated me, the extraordinary machinations that went on in British society on the eve of war.' It was described as an atmospheric conspiracy thriller set against a background of people in England who did not want to go to war with Germany for fear of being annihilated. Bill played the head of one family – a 'Tory sort of Grandee who is also a sort of conservative philosopher.' He described the character as an author who is, 'very much a part of the Tory establishment. He is one of the people who thinks that should we go to war, we will be destroyed, everything we value would be destroyed.' *Glorious 39* premiered at the

Toronto International Film Festival in September 2009 and Bill commented that all those involved in the film were 'very, very pleased with it.'

Also released in 2009 was *Wild Target*, the film he began work on towards the end of 2008. He played Victor Maynard, a middle-aged man and solitary assassin, who despite his reputation for cold and clinical killing, lives to please his formidable mother Louisa (Eileen Atkins). His successful profession is somewhat thwarted when he is drawn to one of his intended victims, Rose (Emily Blunt). He spares her life, unexpectedly acquiring a young orphan, Tony (Rupert Grint) in the process. The two become part of Maynard's life, oblivious to his job, while he has to evade the murdering intentions of his unhappy client (Ferguson), played by Rupert Everett.

Even before the movie was released, Bill was winning praise. Cinema fans' magazine *Empire* wrote: '*Empire* would pay to see the great Bill Nighy in anything, be it a hard-hitting drama about a guy watching paint dry, or a twisting thriller about a guy watching grass grow, or – perhaps most challenging of all – a fly-on-the-wall docudrama about an *Empire* journalist writing news stories about how *Empire* would pay to see the great Bill Nighy in anything. For, with his idiosyncratic line readings and perpetual air of bemusement, as if he's in a joke that nobody else could possibly understand, Nighy brings a freshness and unspeakably cool edge to anything he deigns to be in. He is, frankly, the British Chris Walken.' Unwittingly, the magazine had paid him one of the highest accolades by comparing him to his hero, American actor Walken.

There were other projects in the pipeline too, such as the film *I Was Bono's Doppelganger*. The script was by greatly hailed comedy writing duo, Dick Clement and Ian La Frenais, with additional material by Simon Maxwell and Tony Roche. Bill was lined up to star alongside Irish actor Robert Sheehan, Charlie Cox and his good friends, Romola Garai and Pete Postlethwaite. The music-based comedy recounted the story of how music journalist Neil McCormick dabbles with his brother's chances of becoming a member of the rock band U2. Bill was also rumoured to be starring in romantic comedy *Leap Year* with Amy Adams and Matthew Goode.

Yet another project lined up had Bill starring with Lindsay Duncan in *Weekend*, about a couple whose marriage comes under intense focus when they travel abroad. *Weekend*, written by Hanif Kureishi, was to be directed by Roger Michell and produced by Kevin Loader. The trio were behind the films, *The Mother* and *Venus*. Fitted into all this was a totally new departure for Bill – an appearance in *Statuesque*, one of a series of short silent films shown on Sky One over Christmas. The film told the story of a love triangle between two living statues and the man who admires them daily – unaware that he too is being observed. No, Bill was not the human hero, but one of the statues! A long-term project for Bill was the animated adventure film Rango, in which he provides the voice for 'a rattlesnake with a machine gun!' Bill did his voice-over at the beginning of

2009, but the Gore Verbinski film was not scheduled for release until 2011. Bill's old *Pirates* sparring partner Johnny Depp provides the voice for Rango – at the time of writing, described only vaguely as a 'household pet' who sets off on adventures to find himself. There was also talk of Bill appearing in a John Landis remake of the story of the19th century grave-robbing, murdering duo, Burke and Hare.

No wonder Bill was desperate to take a break. It had been a monumental few years. His success in late middle age still fazed him; often he wondered where it would all lead – and when it would all end. Of course, he can't turn back the clock from being 60, but he would rather be 33 – an age when you are, 'no longer quite as hysterical as when you were young, but you are still a bit more than when you are older…' His philosophy in life is: 'Pay cash, be kind, don't take drugs and pay your taxes.' He pooh-poohs any notion of being a middle-aged sex symbol: 'Am I aware that people have said stuff of that kind? Yes. Do I experience it personally? I couldn't tell you how much I don't. I look in the mirror and remember what I'm supposed to look like. I remember what the prototype was. Now all I see are graphic indications of decline. I'm not knocking the idea, but it's not something I can identify with. I just try not to look in the mirror too much these days.'

When it comes to his acting career, Bill admits there is no dream he has not fulfilled: 'I have had all my dreams but I want to continue to work even though there are no gaps in my work I have to tick off. I would only wish to continue with the kind of material that I have been given.'

Diana moved into the former family home and now shares it with friends, describing it as 'a very good arrangement'. She also confessed to the *Guardian* that she had been propositioned by a married man, but had been unimpressed by his attitude towards marriage – 'You get the heir and the spare, and you do what you like.' Diana had replied: 'Well, I am not old-fashioned enough for that!'

However, there also seemed to be some optimism about her relationship with Bill, when in an interview with *Scotland on Sunday* in June 2009, Diana denied having entered into any new partnerships, mysteriously adding, 'Bill and I have a fine old time. Don't believe what you read in the papers…' But Bill still turned up alone as a guest at the opening night on June 10th of the refurbished Langham Hotel in London. And Diana scotched any idea of a reconciliation in the near future when she said: 'Bill and I don't live together any more, but we're still great friends. We both feel that you can't spend so many years with someone and then just walk away without a backward glance. We know each other far too well for that. Our parting is a reflection of the fact that life changes you and you have to accommodate those changes and allow people to be what they are. That is what being a mature person is all about.' Bill, she said, was still her 'best friend.'

As he reached his landmark birthday, he found comfort that '60 is the new 40'. And he was grateful that the cigarettes, drugs and booze that blighted his former years were no longer part of his life. He looks and feels healthy now that there are no artificial crutches to his wellbeing: 'Everything works, everything seems to still operate. They still keep me in jobs. I can still get into a pair of tight trousers, so what's wrong? I never really think about age. I started later, so I am on a different and exploded schedule to everyone else.'

The late success he is enjoying was unforeseen, but is greatly enjoyable. It is his personal reward for those early years of not knowing where it would all end – or if it was all worth it: 'I never cease to be – honestly, I'm not saying this to be cute. I never cease to be amazed. There's always something, most days, that gets my attention and I just think, "How?" No, you know, I never had, as you may – I never had a plan. And I've improvised most of it. Like most people, I guess. But – no, I had no idea that I would ever – you know, have the kind of professional life that I currently enjoy. How can you see it coming? I had a very recognisable English actor's career which I wasn't complaining about. Lots of things happened to be before the world knew I was around. The whole phenomenon of any kind of public recognition came gradually, so it has been nice and easy. I am glad it didn't happen early as it probably would have killed me…'

Bill is very proud of what daughter Mary, now in her twenties, has achieved. He did not discourage her from going into the same precarious profession as himself (she decided on acting once she abandoned the idea of being an 'international vet' at the age of 9). Mary went on to graduate with first class honours in English from University College London, in 2006. She joined the National Youth Theatre and she appeared in *The Arbitrary Adventures of an Accidental Anarchist.* Following her TV debut in *The Lost Prince*, she was in an episode of 'gardening detectives' drama *Rosemary and Thyme*, an episode of *Spooks* and in America's *Miss Marple* series. There was also an Italian film, *The Fine Art of Love: Mine Ha-Ha*, but perhaps her most high-profile casting to date was as Princesse Lamballe in *Marie Antoinette* (2006) and in the 2009 film, *Tormented* – a 'zom-com' produced by the BBC and Screen West Midlands and released in May.

The movie told the story of Justine Fielding, 'the gorgeous head girl of her plush suburban grammar school' – Fairview High, who has just won a place at Oxford University when in-crowd hunk Alexis asks her out on a date. All seems perfect except Alexis and his circle of friends aren't quite as good as they look. Unfortunately for Bill, work commitments kept him from being among the first to see *Tormented.* He couldn't make the première, which provoked Mary to comment to one journalist: 'You will have to ask him about his excuse.' In 2008, Mary also produced and directed *Player.* Said Bill: 'I haven't discouraged her. It's an honourable profession. She's a wonderful girl and I am very proud of her – and I wouldn't dare give her advice.'

Bill Nighy is a complex, highly insecure man, but a very likeable, amusing, self-effacing, talented one. Writing about himself would have been an uncomfortable, intrusive challenge for him. He has been asked to pen his life story, but always refuses: 'Now I've reached an age where people start to ask you that and I have been asked, I don't know, a dozen times if I'll write a book. I was actually asked the other day if I would sit down with somebody for 21 days and they were offering me an enormous amount of money just to talk into a microphone. But then I realised that I don't want that to happen, because if anyone's going to write a book, I want it to be me.

'Then you think, "Well, why would I be writing the book? What am I writing the book for?" I'm certainly not going to do it for money! If there was a book with my name on it, I would want it to be respectable and I think the only honourable thing for me would be to attempt to be amusing. Also, my nightmare is those books that begin, "I was born under the sign of Taurus on April the 21st" and you just want to kill yourself, then you cut to chapter 5, where they get their first job, you know...'

Naturally, his future plans are to carry on working, to keep music forever in his life and to savour his late success. You get the impression he feels that his career will come to a halt if he does not pursue the many offers that come his way. Towards the end of 2009, Bill was already discussing plans to travel abroad for projects in the coming January and March. But where *will* it end? Who knows, but Bill once said: 'I did always want to retire to west Ireland as my grandmother came from Cork and I always had that romantic idea that I would die on the road home...'

Awards and Credits

BRITISH INDEPENDENT FILM AWARDS

Year	Result	Award	Category
2005	Nominated	British Independent	Best Supporting Actor for *The Constant Gardener* (2005)
2002	Nominated	British Independent	Best Actor for *Lawless Heart* (2001)

ACADEMY OF SCIENCE FICTION, FANTASY & HORROR FILMS, USA

Year	Result	Award	Category
2009	Nominated	Saturn Award	Best Supporting Actor for *Valkyrie* (2008)
2007	Nominated	Saturn Award	Best Supporting Actor for *Pirates of the Caribbean: Dead Man's Chest* (2006)

BAFTA AWARDS

Year	Result	Award	Category
2004	Won	BAFTA Film Award	Best Performance by an Actor in a Supporting Role for *Love Actually* (2003)
2004	Won	BAFTA TV Award	Best Actor for *State of Play* (2003)

BROADCASTING PRESS GUILD AWARDS

Year	Result	Award	Category
2004	Won	BPGA	Best Actor for *State of Play* (2003)
2003	Won	BPGA	Best Actor for *The Lost Prince* (2003)
2003	Won	BPGA	Best Actor in a TV Film for *The Young Visitors* (2003)

EVENING STANDARD BRITISH FILM AWARDS

Year	Result	Award	Category
2004	Won	Peter Sellers Award for Comedy	For *Love Actually* (2003)
1999	Won	Peter Sellers Award for Comedy	For *Still Crazy* (1998)

GOLDEN GLOBES, USA

Year	Result	Award	Category
2007	Won	Golden Globe	Best Performance by an Actor in a Mini-series for *Gideon's Daughter* (2005)
2006	Nominated	Golden Globe	Best Performance by an Actor in a Mini-series for *The Girl in the Café* (2005)

LONDON CRITICS CIRCLE FILM AWARDS

Year	Result	Award	Category
2007	Nominated	ALFS	Best Supporting Actor of the Year for *Notes on a Scandal* (2006)
2004	Won	ALFS	Best Supporting Actor of the Year for *Love Actually* (2003)
2003	Nominated	ALFS	Best Supporting Actor for *Lucky Break* (2002)

LOS ANGELES FILM CRITICS ASSOCIATION AWARD

Year	Result	Award	Category
2004	Won	LAFCA Award	Best Supporting Actor for *Love Actually* (2003)
2004	Won	LAFCA Award	Best Supporting Actor for *AKA* (2002)
2004	Won	LAFCA Award	Best Supporting Actor for *I Capture the Castle* (2003)
2002	Won	LAFCA Award	Best Supporting Actor for *Lawless Heart* (2001)

MTV MOVIE AWARDS

Year	Result	Award	Category
2007	Nominated	MTV Movie Award	Best Villain for *Pirates of the Caribbean: Dead Man's Chest* (2006)

PHOENIX FILM CRITICS SOCIETY AWARDS

Year	Result	Award	Category
2004	Nominated	PFCS	Best Ensemble Acting for *Love Actually* (2003) Shared with whole cast

ROYAL TELEVISION SOCIETY, UK

Year	Result	Award	Category
2004	Nominated	RTS	Best Actor – Male for *State of Play* (2003)

SATELLITE AWARDS

Year	Result	Award	Category
2006	Won	Satellite Award	Best Actor in a Mini-series for *Gideon's Daughter* (2005)
2005	Won	Golden Satellite	Best Actor in a Supporting Role in a Mini-series for *The Lost Prince* (2003)
2004	Nominated	Golden Satellite	Best Performance by an Actor in a Supporting Role, Comedy or Musical for *Love Actually* (2003)
1999	Nominated	Golden Satellite	Best Performance by an Actor in a Motion Picture Comedy or Musical for *Still Crazy* (1998)

TEEN CHOICE AWARDS

Year	Result	Award	Category
2007	Won	TCA	Choice Movie: Villain for *Pirates of the Caribbean: At World's End* (2007)
2006	Won	TCA	Choice Movie: Sleazebag for *Pirates of the Caribbean: Dead Man's Chest* (2006)

OTHER

2001 Won Olivier Award for Best Stage Actor for *Blue/Orange*
1996 Won Barclays Theatre Award for Best Stage *Actor for Skylight*

BIG SCREEN/SMALL SCREEN CREDITS

Rango (2011): Rattlesnake
Astro Boy (2009): (voice) Dr. Elefun
G-Force (2009): Leonard Saber
Wild Target (2009): Victor Maynard
Glorious 39 (2009): Alexander
The Boat That Rocked (2009): Quentin
aka *Radio Rock Revolution* (Germany)
Underworld: Rise of the Lycans (2009): Viktor
Valkyrie (2008): General Friedrich Olbricht
Slapper (2008): Arnold Percy
Coping Strategies (2008): Julian
A Fox's Tale (UK) (2008): (voice) Ringmaster
Pirates of the Caribbean: At World's End (2007): Davy Jones
Hot Fuzz (2007): Met Chief Inspector
Notes on a Scandal (2006): Richard Hart
Flushed Away (2006): (voice) Whitey
Stormbreaker (2006): Alan Blunt
Pirates of the Caribbean: Dead Man's Chest (2006): Davy Jones
Underworld: Evolution (2006): Viktor
Gideon's Daughter (2006) (TV): Gideon Warner
The Constant Gardener (2005): Sir Bernard Pellegrin
The Girl in the Café (2005) (TV): Lawrence

The Hitchhiker's Guide to the Galaxy (2005): Slartibartfast
The Magic Roundabout (2005) (voice: English version): Dylan the Rabbit
Enduring Love (2004): Robin
He Knew He Was Right (2004) (TV mini-series): Colonel Osborne
Shaun of the Dead (2004): Philip
Animated Tales of the World (1 episode, 2002): Tiger
Life Beyond the Box: Norman Stanley Fletcher (2003) (TV): Narrator
The Young Visiters (2003) (TV): Earl of Clincham
Canterbury Tales (1 episode: *The Wife of Bath*, 2003): James
Underworld (2003): Viktor
Love Actually (2003): Billy Mack
State of Play (6 episodes, 2003): Cameron Foster
The Lost Prince (2003): Stamfordham
I Capture the Castle (2003): James Mortmain
Ready When You Are, Mr McGill (2003)(TV): Phil Parish
Auf Wiedersehen, Pet (6 episodes, 2002): Jeffrey Grainger
The Inspector Lynley Mysteries (1 episode, 2002): Lockwood
AKA (2002): Uncle Louis Gryffoyn
Lucky Break (2001): Roger 'Rog' Chamberlain/King George III in *Show*
Lawless Heart (2001): Dan
Blow Dry (2001): Ray (Raymond) Robertson
Longitude (2000)(TV): Lord Sandwich
The Magic of Vincent (2000): Peter Saunders
The Journey Back (2000)(voice: TV)
Kiss Me Kate (3 episodes, 1999–2000): Iain Cameron
Guest House Paradiso (1999): Mr Johnson
People Like Us (1 episode, 1999): Will Rushmore
The Canterbury Tales (2 episodes, 1998–2000): The Merchant
Still Crazy (1998): Ray Simms
The Bass Player (1998): Count Bibuloff
Leaving London (1998)(voice: TV)
FairyTale: A True Story (1997): Edward Gardner
Kavanagh QC (1 episode, 1997): Giles Culpepper QC
Insiders (2 episodes, 1997): Mark Gordon
Treasure Island (1997): Long John Silver
Testament: The Bible in Animation (1 episode, 1996): Belshazzar

Indian Summer (1996): Tristan
True Blue (1996): Jeremy Saville
Wycliffe (1 episode, 1994): David Cleeve
God's Messenger (1994 mini-series): George Fox/William Gaskell/ JohnWesley/Charles Burton
The Maitlands (1 episode, 1993): *Don't Leave Me This Way* (1993)(TV): John Tracey
Peak Practice (1 episode, 1993): Alan Sinclair
P.D. James: Unnatural Causes (1993)(TV): Oliver Latham
Being Human (1993): Julian
Eye of the Storm (1993)(TV mini-series): Tom Frewen
A Masculine Ending (1992) (TV): John Tracey
Chillers (1 episode, 1992): Tom Dickenson
Absolute Hell (1991)(TV): Hugh Marriner
Antonia and Jane (1991): Howard Nash
The Men's Room (5 episodes, 1991): Prof Mark Carleton
Boon (1 episode, 1991): Steve Reeves
Bergerac (1 episode, 1991): Barry
Making News (1990)(TV series): Sam Courtney
Mack the Knife (1990): Tiger Brown
The Phantom of the Opera (1989): Martin Barton
Storyboard (1 episode, 1989): Sam
Writing on the Wall (1990)(TV): Brill
Muzzy (1987) (voice: TV): Judge Gilbert
The Last Place on Earth (4 episodes, 1985): Cecil Meares
Hitler's S.S.: Portrait in Evil (1985)(TV): Helmut Hoffmann
Thirteen at Dinner (1985)(TV): Ronald Marsh
Crown Court (1 episode, 1984): Lee Sinclair
The Little Drummer Girl (1984)(Theatre Company): Al
Jemima Shore Investigates (1 episode, 1983)
Curse of the Pink Panther (1983): ENT Doctor
Reilly: Ace of Spies (1 episode, 1983): Goschen
Minder (1 episode, 1982): Oates
Waveband (1982): Cast Member
Play for Tomorrow: Easter 2016 (1982): Connor Mullan
Eye of the Needle (1981): Squadron Leader Blenkinsop

Agony (7 episodes, 1980–81): Vincent Fish
Fox (2 episodes, 1980): Colin Street
Little Lord Fauntleroy (1980): Officer
BBC2 Playhouse: Standing in for Henry (1980): Bruno
Play For Today (3 episodes, 1978–82)
   1. Soldiers Talking Cleanly (1978): Bill
   2. Dreams of Leaving (1980): William
   3. Under the Skin (1982): Dave
The Bitch (1979) [Bill's character was cut!]: Delivery Boy
Death Watch (1979): Young Man
Fat (1979): Nick
Deasey (1 episode, 1979): Deasey
Softly, Softly (1 episode, 1976): Albert Blake

SOUNDTRACKS

The Magic Roundabout (2005) Performer: 'You Really Got Me'
Love Actually (2003) Performer: 'Christmas Is All Around'

ON-SCREEN PERSONAL APPEARANCES/NARRATION

Rove Live (2009)
The ONE Show (2009)
Sunday AM (2008)
Time Shift (2007)
Spy Stories (2007)
Entertainment Tonight (2007)
HypaSpace (2007)
The 64th Annual Golden Globe Awards (2007)
Horizon (2006 – Narrator)
HBO First Look (2006)
Down the Loo: The Making of Flushed Away (2006)
Richard & Judy (2006)
The Armstrongs (2006 – Narrator)
The Armstrongs: The Movie (2006 – Narrator)
Meerkat Manor (2005–06 – Narrator)
'The Hitchhiker's Guide to the Galaxy' (2005)
The Magic of Music (2005)

Magical Voices (2005)
British Academy Television Awards 2005 (2005)
Inside 'The Hitchhiker's Guide to the Galaxy' (2005)
The Paul O'Grady Show (2005)
The Evening Standard British Film Awards (2005)
Touts on Tour: TV (2004)
1st Annual Directors Guild of Great Britain Awards (2004)
Teaching Awards (2004)
Live on the Night (2004 – Narrator)
Lucy's Cam (2004)
Liquid News (2004)
Parkinson (2004)
Parkinson: Tribute to Peter Ustinov (2004 – Narrator/contributor)
The BAFTA TV Awards 2004 (2004)
1st Annual Directors Guild of Great Britain DGGB Awards (2004)
Shaun of the Dead: EPK Featurette (2004)
Don't Crash: The Documentary of the Making of the Movie of the Book of the Radio Series of Live on the Night (2004 – Narrator)
BBC Breakfast (five appearances, 2003–2005)
The Morning Show (2003)
Grumpy Old Men (4 episodes – 2003)
Life Beyond the Box (2003 – Narrator)
The Office Christmas Party (2003 – Narrator)
The King, The Kaiser and the Tsar (for *The Lost Prince*) (2003)
Live Lunch (2001)
Look North (two appearances – 2001/1996)
Jim'll Fix It (shown on set of *Bleak House*)(1982)
On the Town (clip of *Illuminations* stage play)(1980)

THEATRE

The Vertical Hour as Oliver Lucas, Music Box Theatre, New York 2006
Speak Now as Timmy, Traverse Edinburgh 2004
Collateral Damage II as Performer, National Theatre (London) 2003
Collateral Damage V as Performer, National Theatre (London) 2003
Blue/Orange as Robert, Royal National Theatre (London) 2000
A Kind of Alaska as Doctor, Donmar Warehouse Theatre (London) 1998

Skylight as Tom Sergeant, Vaudeville Theatre (London) 1997
The Seagull as Trigorin, National Theatre: Olivier (London) 1994
Arcadia as Bernard Nightingale, National Theatre: Lyttelton (London) 1993
Betrayal as Performer, Almeida Theatre (London) 1991
Mean Tears as Julian, National Theatre: Cottesloe (London) 1987
King Lear as Edgar, National Theatre: Olivier (London) 1986
Pravda as Eaton Sylvestra, National Theatre: Olivier (London) 1985
Map of the World as Stephen Andrews, National Theatre: Lyttleton (London) 1983
Illuminations as Gorman, Lyric Theatre Hammersmith (London) 1980
The Warp as Performer, Institute of Contemporary Arts (London) 1979
Occupy! as Performer, Everyman Theatre (Liverpool) 1976

OLDER WORK

The Milk Train Does Not Stop Here Any More as Performer, Watermill Theatre (Newbury)
Entertaining Mr. Sloane as Sloane, Gateway Chester (Chester)
Comings and Goings as Vernon Crouch, Hampstead Theatre (London)
Freedom of the City as Skinner, Everyman Theatre (Liverpool)
Rosencrantz & Guildenstern are Dead as Rosencrantz, Cambridge Arts (Cambridge)
Under New Management as Harold, Everyman Theatre (Liverpool)
The Immoralist as Performer, Hampstead Theatre (London)
Landscape and Silence as Performer, Gateway Chester (Chester)
Epitaph for George Dillon as Performer, Guildford School (Guildford, Surrey)

AUDIOBOOKS

Bill is an ambassador or Silksoundbooks, a website where you can buy your favourite books read by your favourite actors (www.silksoundbooks.com). The first title available read by him is *The Dupin Mysteries* by Edgar Allan Poe which was released in July).

He has also read various audiobooks:
Sleeping Cruelty, Lynda La Plante. Audio Cassette (September 2000)
Short Stories: The Ultimate Modern Collection. Audio CD (October 2005). CSA WORD

Our Mutual Friend, Charles Dickens. Audio Cassette (March 1998). BBC Audiobooks

War and Peace, Leo Tolstoy. Audio Cassette (February 1998). Penguin Audiobooks

You Magazine Short Story Collection, read by Janet McTeer and Bill Nighy. Audio Cassette ((February 1996). CSA WORD

The Diary of Samuel Pepys: A Radio 4 Classic Serial, Audio Cassette (January 1995). BBC Audiobooks

Kolymsky Heights, Lionel Davidson. Audio Cassette (May 1995). Random House Audiobooks

Spooked, Hooked, The Bargain, Handle with Care, Murder in Mind, Down Came a Spider, A Lucky Charm and Co, Bob Read, Bill Nighy (Narrator). Audio Cassette (August 1995). Hodder Arnold H&S

Acknowledgements

Bill Nighy Fan Site: www.billnighy.info
The Bill Nighy Experience: www.billnighy.net
Tiscali: www.tiscali.co.uk
Rotten Tomatoes: www.rottentomatoes.com
The Numbers, Box Office Data: www.the-numbers.com
Filmbug: www.filmbug.com
Times Online: www.timesonline.co.uk
The *Guardian*: www.guardian.co.uk
Daily Telegraph/Sunday Telegraph: www.telegraph.co.uk
London *Evening Standard*: www.thisislondon.co.uk
Daily Mail: www.dailymail.co.uk
News of the World: www.newsoftheworld.co.uk
Scotland on Sunday: www.scotlandonsunday.scotsman.com
Irish Independent: www.independent.ie
Who's Dated Who?: www.whosdatedwho.com
IMDb: www.imdb.com
Yahoo! Movies: www.movies.yahoo.com
Movie Gun Services LLC: www.moviegunservices.com
Australian Broadcasting Corporation
Easy Living Magazine
Time Out
Radio Times
Empire Magazine

Hollywood Reporter

Variety

New York Daily News

New York Times

Sydney Morning Herald

Seattle Weekly

Philadelphia Enquirer

Dorset Echo

BBC Films

Paul Scott, *Daily Mail*

Lester Middlehurst, *Daily Mail*

Lewis Panther, *News of the World*

Lynn Barber, *Telegraph*

Sue Arnold, *Guardian*

Dominic Wills, *Tiscali*

Matthew Bond, Mail on Sunday

Nick Curtis, *London Evening Standard*

Peter Bradshaw, *Guardian*

David Smith, *Observer*

Kathryn Flett, *Guardian*

Susan Daly, *Irish Independent*

Ariel Leve, *Sunday Times*

Aidan Smith, *The Scotsman*

Caroline Shearing, *Telegraph*

Kerry O'Brien, *Australian Broadcasting Corporation*

Garth Pearce

Stuart Prebble

Paul Fischer

Rachel Quarrell

Sean Nelson

Printed in Great Britain
by Amazon

15245593R00166